Standing on His Promises—

Then and Now

Joan M. Blake

Standing on His Promises—*Then and Now*
by Joan M. Blake

ISBN 978-0-9814609-9-4

Published by:
KEY TO LIFE PUBLISHING COMPANY
P.O. BOX 190971 • BOSTON, MA 02119

Key to Life
PUBLISHING COMPANY

Printed in the United States of America.

Dedication

I dedicate this book to my daughter, Monique—
a humble, hardworking woman, devoted wife,
and mother of three. Through her years in the
school system, she has touched the lives of
countless children and families in need.

Despite the challenges, she persevered, earning
her doctorate in education while expecting her
second child. May God continue to guide and
bless you in the years to come.

Table of Contents

Table of Contents *(CONTINUED)*

Preface

I n every life there are times of joy and times of crisis. During times of crisis, we face emotional issues and other obstacles that inhibit our growth, hold us captive, and keep us from walking in our destiny and achieving our purposes, purposes that God set for us before the foundation of the world. Such obstacles might include family issues, job issues, church issues, or dealing with a special needs child or adult. The list can go on.

I felt that I should update you on how my family has evolved since the writing of *Standing on His Promises: Finding Comfort, Hope, and Purpose in the Midst of Your Storm* in 2007, so you, too, can have comfort, hope, and purpose in the midst of your storm. While some storms have passed, my storms did not leave completely. What happened, instead, was I learned to embrace joy in the midst of my pain.

Standing on His Promises: Then and Now describes my journey leaving Trinidad to come to America alone, going to college, getting married, having a family, experiencing crisis, but enjoying our lives in the midst of turmoil. I sought God and He gave me strength, comfort, hope, and purpose during my darkest hours. I honor, praise, and thank Him for the wisdom and insights that He imparted to me throughout the course of writing and revising this book, without which this book could not be possible.

This book is written for women of all ages, nationalities, colors, cultures, religions, for stay-at-home moms, women in positions of power, business owners, students, single parents, single women, pastors, evangelists, and lay leaders, from all walks of life, who find themselves in the midst of pain and do not know where to turn.

The purpose of this book is to give women encouragement and hope in their everyday lives, to enable them to trust and rest in God and to experience peace and joy regardless of the situations they face. Peace and rest come when one makes a conscious decision to surrender all of life's challenges and fears to God, to draw near to Him in prayer and praise, and to thank Him continually for His mighty acts. God loves and cares for you. Most importantly, God is sovereign, and He knows and controls every situation you face, from its inception. With tender hands, He is carrying you through your difficulty; with His grace, He is giving you the power to face and to overcome your challenges and fears and to press on toward your destiny. God promises never to leave or forsake you (Josh. 1:5).

I have dedicated this book to my daughter Monique, who has shown strength and determination throughout her life as a devoted wife and mother.

I thank my husband, Carl, for his love and consideration, because over the years he has shared the responsibility of raising our four children, who are now adults, providing for us, and being there for us in good times as well as in challenging times. Carl is a man of integrity, compassionate, and hopeful. God had a purpose for creating this man with patience, stability, and being a backbone for our entire family. Carl continues to remain calm under unusual circumstances and continues to support me and give me the freedom and encouragement to be all that God has called me to be.

Tony, our older son, has been a great listener and encourager. As a husband and father, he demonstrates virtues of love, patience, kindness, gentleness, and compassion in his family as well as in ours. I am grateful to God for him. Reese, our younger son, has shown love, support, encouragement, and compassion for his sister Jo-An. His compassion extends to those who are disadvantaged. I thank Reese for his willingness to share with others how God has restored his life.

Monique has been a joy to me. I thank God for birthing patience in her, for the unique gifts with which He has blessed her, and for how she has used these gifts for His glory. I am grateful for her love, comfort, continual feedback, support, and friendship over the years. She has also been a moral support to her sister Jo-An.

Jo-An has been God's testing ground to help me understand what God's unconditional love is, to show me that God is no respecter of persons, and that He loves Jo-An just as much as He loves anyone else. My experience with Jo-An has helped me understand what patience is and how God has been patient with me. God has helped me to live a life of faith in the midst of pain and revealed to me what He can do in the life of an individual when I show the same level of unconditional love to another human being that He has shown to me.

Thanks to Anika Thomas, who supplied me with additional information on the foods and juices of Trinidad and Tobago, and to the many friends and family members who have supported and encouraged me.

Because of the personal nature of this book, I have decided to comply with my family's wishes to use middle names for our daughters and nicknames for our sons in order to protect their identities.

I pray that, as you read this book, God will pour out so many blessings on you that you will not have room to receive them. I pray that you will be free from the stains of your past and from current situations that hold you hostage, and that you will walk as children of God, renewed in your mind and set free by the blood of the Lamb.

1 Living in Trinidad

I was born on the island of Trinidad and Tobago, a small dual-island Caribbean nation in the West Indies, 6.8 miles off the coast of Northeastern Venezuela. My father, John, and my mother, Agnes, had six children: five daughters and one son, plus two older brothers on my mom's side from a previous marriage. I had no idea that my life would change to the point that everyone in the family would look to me for guidance. We were an average, working-class family, not having much but looking eagerly to receive life's unexpected blessings.

As of 2021, of the country's 1.526 million inhabitants, most (96%) reside on the island of Trinidad and the remaining (4%) in Tobago. The island of Trinidad and Tobago consists of various ethnic groups: East Indians (originally from Northern India) represent about 35.4%, blacks 34.2%, mixed races 15.3%, African/East Indian 7.7%, other 1.3%, and unspecified 6.2%. The religions are as follows: 26% are Roman Catholics; 22.5% are Hindus; 7.8% are Anglicans; 7.2% are Baptists, 6.8% are Pentecostals, 5.8% are Muslims; 4% are Seventh-day Adventists, 5.8% are other Christians, other denominations are 10.8%, 1.4% are unspecified, and those with no religion are 1.9%.The official language of the island is English. Colloquial language spoken is reflective of Trinidad and Tobago's European and African heritage. Other languages include Hindi, French-Creole, and Spanish *(Statistics derived from the 2021 census and other publicly available data sources)*.

The island's economy is dependent on tourism and natural gas, but it also supplies food and beverages as well as cement to the Caribbean region.

Trinidad and Tobago cover an area of 1,981square miles, with hills and mountains in plain view. It is surrounded by water, scenic beaches, and palm trees, which invite relaxation for tourists and residents alike. It is home to cricket tournaments and carnival celebrations. The residents of the island stage a pre-Lenten carnival, a two-day celebration on the streets of Port-of-Spain, in early February of each year. People dress in various costumes and display floats of all kinds that they have made themselves over the past year. Calypso singers and children's carnival contests precede the actual carnival celebrations.

1

The island's landscape is covered with naturally grown, perennial tropical plants with flowers of various shades of pink, yellow, orange, red, and green, pleasing to the eye. There are also fruit trees, which include mango, plum, chenet, tamarind, citrus, papaya, peewah, pineapple, pomerac, pommecythere, sapodilla, soursop, bananas, plantain, passion fruit, coconut, avocado, barbadeen, and guava. Vegetable gardens grow corn, tomatoes, cabbages, cucumbers, bodi, ochroes, lettuce, patchoi, sweet peppers, celery, cauliflower, sorrel, breadfruit, and pumpkin as well as root vegetables, such as dasheen, cassava, eddoes, yam, tania, and sweet potatoes.

An array of delicacies and juices are made from the fruits. For example, the curried mango chutney dish and stewed and red mango are made from the mango fruit; jelly, jam, and cheese are made from the guava fruit; and juices are made from mango, coconut, guava, papaya, passion fruit, and pineapple.

Main dishes include callaloo, coo-coo, pelau, rice and peas, cornmeal dumplings, roti, fried or stewed fish (king fish, red fish, shark, and others), chicken, duck, turkey, fried and roast bakes, buljol, accra, and boiled or fried plantain.

Callaloo is made from dasheen leaf or spinach, is cooked and blended with ochroes and seasonings into a thick, smooth, dark-green paste, lightly salted, rich in aroma and appetizing. It is occasionally cooked with crab meat. Coo-coo, made with cornmeal, ochroes, coconut milk, butter, salt, and pepper, is pale yellow, mushy, and has a mild taste. Pelau is rice cooked with pigeon peas (dried green peas), seasonings, chopped chicken or beef, and coconut milk, while the rice and peas dish is sometimes prepared without meat. Burned sugar colors the rice, peas, and the meat giving them a dark brown appearance. The rice and peas are firmly cooked; herbal and other seasonings create a Mediterranean aroma and delicious taste. Cornmeal dumplings are firm and pale yellow. The dough is cut into small shapes to make small dumplings for soups or larger shapes for a meal of dumplings and codfish. Roti, an Indian dish, is a thin flour wrap that is prepared in different ways: as a dhalpuri roti made with split peas, saffron, and other ingredients or as a plain roti or buss-up-shut roti, which is broken up into sections. The roti wraps are soft, off-white in color, lightly salted, and filled with curried and seasoned chicken, beef, goat or vegetables. The yellow fillings are juicy, mouth-watering, hot, and flavorsome. Buljol is made from dried codfish which is washed and stripped and mixed with oil, onions, tomatoes, garlic, sweet peppers, or pimentos. The dish is oily, lightly salted, spicy, soft, and tasty. Accra is a spicy fish dish that is lightly salted, crunchy, and greasy, but delicious. It is also made from dried codfish but is put into a batter of flour with seasonings and cooked in oil.

Fried and roast bakes are formed from the dough that is prepared with baking powder and are cooked until they become light brown; dough is fried in oil to make crispy fried bakes and baked to make moist roasted bakes. A fried bake resembles a bun and a roast bake resembles a large pizza without the toppings. All meats and fish are highly seasoned with herbs that leave a fresh aroma and mouth-watering taste. Boiled or fried plantains resemble bananas but are longer; they are yellow, soft when cooked or fried, and complement main dishes.

Holiday favorites include sweetbread, black cake, ginger beer, sorrel, mauby, and ponche de crème. Sweetbread is made with flour, grated coconut, mixed fruit, spices, margarine, raisins, currants, milk, vanilla essence, baking powder, and sugar and cooked until it is slightly brown; it has a sweet taste and the spices give it a wonderful aroma. Black cake is made with flour, eggs, butter, sugar, spices, rum or wine, lime peel, vanilla essence, cinnamon, and baking powder, with raisins, currants, prunes, and cherries grinded together. The browning liquid made from sugar colors the cake black, and the ingredients and spices create a sweet, rich, moist, and delicious taste. Ginger beer is made from grated ginger and other spices, which give it a light yellow appearance, and leaves a burning sensation in one's mouth. Sorrel, which is a deep red, sweetened, but a slightly sour drink, is made from a flower that is dried after its seeds are removed and boiled with certain spices. Mauby drink, pale brown in color, mild and bittersweet, is made from the bark of a tree which is boiled with spices. Ponche de crème, made with eggs, milk, rum, lime, angostura bitters, and other flavorings, is a thick, creamy drink similar to eggnog but with a fruity flavor.

The climate of Trinidad is usually hot and sunny, about 89 degrees, with the exception of intermittent rainy periods between June and December. The heat mixed with gusts of wind sweep through the air making one feel joyful and rejuvenated. People use umbrellas to ward off the sun and dress casually in short-sleeved shirts, dresses, skirts, pants, and shorts.

I lived in the village of Morvant, situated outside Port-of-Spain. Throughout the day, one could hear a mother calling for her children to do chores, and the children, engulfed in their play of jump rope or cricket, pretending not to hear her beckoning calls.

The neighbors were poor or working-class people who reached out to each other. There was never a day that Miss Peterson did not say, "Good morning, Mrs. Moses. How'd you do?" My mother's reply would always be, "I am so-so yes, darling."

On occasions, my mother would talk to a neighbor near the fence while hanging out her clothes to dry, or someone would drop by our home and say to my dad, "How'd you do, ole man?" My dad would play a game of chess with his guest, and before the evening ended, there would be several people playing chess, or "draft," as we called it. A neighbor might visit because she needed flour, tea leaves to make tea for her children, or an onion to season her meat, and my mother always provided her with what she needed.

When I was a young child, my mother and father always wanted me to confess which of them was my favorite parent. I never admitted that my father was my favorite for fear that my mother might become jealous, but my mother knew. I loved my father more because he was calmer than my mother, and I could get a word through to him. My mother was boisterous, and, although she worked hard at home and was kind and caring to her children, she never took time to get to know us. She never took time to relax; she worked continually. From a young age, I knew what I wanted. I was very independent and opinionated but also obedient to my parents, knowing that was the better way to go. I wanted to please my parents and to get their approval, so I attended church and excelled in school. Being their first daughter, I felt a responsibility to be all that they wanted me to be.

I was eight years old when I celebrated my first communion at a local Catholic church. It was the most important day of my life. Although I was not sure what it all meant, I knew it was a happy, momentous occasion, one that would change my life forever as I learned to love God, obey His commandments, and live a life worthy of Him. I wore a white nylon gown, a veil, and a crown, and, with hands clasped, received Holy Communion for the first time during Mass at a Roman Catholic church nearby. After the Mass, I visited my neighbors and received their blessings which meant a great deal to me. My mother set up an altar in our small living room, which she decorated with a linen cloth, two tall candles, and a rosary. I sat in front of the altar, recited the rosary during the day, and said short prayers. From an early age, I learned the discipline of going before God. At bedtime, I would continue this discipline by kneeling by my bed and praying to God. I would often fall asleep before my prayer ended, and my mother would gently steer me into my bed.

My mother cleaned, cooked, washed our clothes by hand, and did all the ironing. I vowed that, when I became older and able, I would help her with household chores. On rainy days, I wore my father's rain boots in the wet, muddy backyard as I did my daily chores of feeding the poultry: ducks, fowls, turkeys, and chickens. At night, we would secure the poultry in handmade houses in groups of six to protect them from animals waiting to make them their prey. Squirrels and birds also had their little hideouts in their cages. I would hold my breath so as not to inhale the stench coming from the houses as I opened them to change the beds and to give the animals food and water.

Raising poultry was customary for families in my country. It was a joy to hear the "gobbling" noise of the turkeys and to see and hear the ducks flap their wings as they bathed in the pond we had made. I got the chance to see turkeys, fowls, and ducks give birth to their little ones. As the time drew near for their babies to be born, their eggs would become darker and, little by little, the babies would break through the eggs. Sometimes, I would help in the birth process by breaking just a piece of an eggshell. Joy came when, for example, six yellow ducklings were born and were strong enough to walk to the pond in single file behind their mother in order to learn the skills of bathing, eating, and flying. For Christmas, we would choose the fattest turkey, duck, or fowl or a combination of any two kinds of poultry for our dinner. I would sadly help my mother butcher them in preparation for the holiday meal.

As a young girl, I loved the outdoors and enjoyed playing typical games for girls my age, including hopscotch and jump rope. However, I did not participate in a sport at school. In my teenage years, my parents allowed me to go on monthly picnics with friends at the Royal Botanic Garden in Trinidad, which is located in Port-of-Spain just north of the Queen's Park Savannah. I enjoyed the beauty of the flowers, the birds, and the hills. I often climbed the hills and would experience leg cramps afterward, to the point that I would cry from the pain.

When I was old enough, I kept my vow and helped my mother around the house, cooking and cleaning, ironing clothes, and doing house painting during the holiday season. I particularly enjoyed gardening: planting a seed, watching the seed grow into a plant, and seeing a whole crop evolve from one seed. We planted corn, tomatoes, spinach, dasheen, and other vegetables. We also had mango trees, and I loved to jump up and pick a mango.

As a teenager, I loved both learning and teaching others, so I tutored my cousin and our neighbor's two children in English and mathematics for free. I particularly enjoyed the routine of attending school, going to the library after school, and taking examinations and wondering if I had passed them. When I became overwhelmed with studies, my father relieved me of house duties by hiring a helper to assist my mother. From that time forward, school became my manner of life and my passport to my independence and freedom. My parents encouraged me to further my studies and go abroad. I knew the day would come when I would graduate from home.

2 Leaving Home

Going abroad was no small matter to me. It meant the possibility of going to college, landing a job, and creating an opportunity for my family members and myself. I could have relinquished the idea of going abroad, but what did I have to lose? Staying in Trinidad meant competing with the brightest students for a seat at either the University of Trinidad or Jamaica. Then, there was the difficulty of obtaining a job right out of the university and the fact that my father was not able to afford the cost of a college education. My father, advanced in years and the breadwinner, was a shipping clerk who checked in daily for work at the wharf and would return home empty-handed. On those disappointing days, my mother would comfort him with: "John, don't worry; God will see us through." When I told friends, family, and neighbors that I was going abroad, they packed into our two-bedroom home to give me their farewell hugs and best wishes.

Ms. Thelma, our neighbor across the street, said, "Joan, yuh parents are depending on yuh to do well; don't let dem down, now. When yuh in trouble, don't forget to call on duh name of God, yuh hear?"

I was tired of listening to people's advice and, worse yet, their expectations. My thoughts were, *"Are these people setting me up for failure?"*

However, I humbly took their advice and, with mixed feelings, pictured myself in a world with newly found freedom, leaving the old world illuminated by all of its beauty and yet darkened by our parents' inherent structure and control and the subsequent boredom under which we children lived.

I was leaving Trinidad and Tobago, the place of my birth, where I had grown up with the security and love of my parents, extended family, and neighbors, a community of people who loved and cared for me, appreciated me, and understood me and was going to a place where I knew no one. The thought of leaving everything and everyone behind was frightening, but I pretended that I was going on an adventure, which initiated excitement in me and readied me for what lay ahead.

My parents encouraged me, tailored warm pajamas and two-piece skirt-suits, and gave me 500 US dollars. I did the needed research and decided that I wanted to go to Boston to live, work, and attend college.

I learned of a residence located in the South End of Boston and applied for a room there. They referred me to a YWCA, located on Clarendon Street, where I stayed temporarily until the residence had a vacancy.

My flight to the United States was my first plane ride, so I was a bit nervous. I prayed at times and put my fingers in my ears to ward off the funny feeling I experienced when the plane was either ascending or descending. At night, sparkling lights from the skyscrapers produced picturesque and scenic views of New York and Boston.

"This is certainly different," I thought.

I arrived in Boston, safe and sound, on October 27, 1968, after a seven-hour flight that I was glad had ended. I got to the luggage pickup and suddenly realized that I had no one to receive me. I walked briskly but cautiously to the front gate and hailed a taxi to the local YWCA, where I was staying temporarily. Back on the island, I had heard strange stories of bad things happening to good people, and that thought frightened me somewhat. I thought the best way to handle the driver was to talk to him a lot. I proceeded to ask him, "Are you from here?"

He said, "No," and continued to drive, paying close attention to the steering wheel and the tunnel that we were approaching.

I continued, "Where are you from, then?"

"I am from Haiti," he said. "I studied in Haiti and came here to make it better for my family there."

"Wow, I came here to do the same," I responded. "This is my first time traveling, and I am looking forward to my stay here. The place I am staying is on Clarendon Street."

"At last, I'm in America!" I exclaimed. I was going to the United States to work and attend college. I had not yet applied for a job or college and had no idea how my plans would materialize. However, I was determined to persevere and attain my goals, regardless of how long it would take me to achieve them.

Before long, we got to my destination, and I was safe. I got out of the taxi, thanked the driver for a safe journey, paid him, giving him a $2 tip for his service, and proceeded to the front desk. I approached the front desk, gave my name, paid the balance I owed, was handed my key, and was told to go to the seventh floor. The women at the desk were friendly. The first question one asked me was, "Do you sing?"

I said, "Oh no, I wish I did."

Her reply was, "You have a beautiful voice, and I like your accent too."

"Thank you."

"Do they speak English in Trinidad?"

"Yes, we do. People believe that we speak another language because of the different ethnic backgrounds present on our island. There are Blacks, Indians, Chinese, Spanish, Whites, mixed races, and other nationalities."

After speaking with the receptionist, I took the elevator to my room. The ride in the elevator seemed endless. There was no one in there but me. As I exited the elevator, I shuddered at the thought of walking down the dark, gloomy hallway, passing closed doors and not even hearing the sound of voices. I grappled with my loneliness. I opened the door and anxiously and eagerly walked into my room, not knowing what I would find there. The room was small, neat, and comfortable, with a twin bed, a small bureau, a telephone, a desk, and a chair, but with little room to walk around. I left the room with my key in hand for a minute or two, hoping that by chance I would come across someone in the hallway, but, to my utter disappointment, there was no one—no Mammy, no Daddo to talk to, no neighbors to call out to. No one. For the next two or three minutes, fear engulfed me. I decided to put the bolt on the door for protection, go under the covers, and cry myself to sleep.

Thoughts flooded my mind. *"I came to America to better myself, to further my education, to help my parents, my siblings, to make a way for all of us. There is no need to cry. This is your first day in America, give yourself time."* Just then, I thought of a better way to deal with my fear. *"What do I have to lose if I pray?"* I thought—so I prayed to God. I do not remember saying too much…

3 Starting Over

After two weeks, I moved from the YWCA on Clarendon Street to the residence where I had pre-registered. The residence was a large community building with brightly lit single rooms conveniently located in the South End of Boston not far from an MBTA stop. The front foyer was beautifully carpeted and included an array of large green plants, which enhanced its beauty. The residence was an exciting place to live; I was able to live alone, enjoy my privacy, and yet, be in the company of other women. It gave me an opportunity to learn new things and meet new people. I learned how to live in a community and gained friendships that I had no idea would last for a lifetime.

The residence afforded us, single women, comfort and a safe environment to live in. We had breakfast and dinner, shared the laundry room, and had Sunday tea and brunch together. The Sunday tea was special; tea was served at 3 p.m. in special chinaware. We were not allowed to wear slacks for tea or dinner. We had a curfew of 11 p.m. during the week and 12 p.m. on weekends. It was interesting to watch and admire other women as they went to the next level in their relationships, as their dates brought flowers for them and took them out to dinner. On the weekends, finding a place to eat was challenging as we did not have meals at the residence. Some of the women chose to go to a restaurant a few miles away, go downtown to eat, purchase light snacks from the tiny mom and pop stores nearby, or go on dinner dates on Sunday evenings, traveling alone or with a friend if one was left.

I used the $500 US that my father had given me carefully and wisely. I quickly learned the subway by trial and error and, before long, was applying for jobs. I applied to banks because they were more accessible by train, or within walking distance, and easier for me to secure an entry-level position.

Five weeks later, I obtained a clerical position at a local bank in Boston. I had been at the job no more than a month when I looked up and saw Carl taking a tour of the very bank where I was working. I recognized his six-foot figure, long gait, serious facial expression, and calm composure. We had been close friends in Trinidad, dated for a short time, and then I left to come to America. I was surprised to see him. I stared at him long and hard, then looked down and continued doing my work. I looked up again and realized he was coming my way. His eyes and mine met, and I knew at that moment that God had ordained our meeting. Carl came over to my desk, and I remember saying, "I did not know that you were in Boston. When did you come, and how long are you staying?"

With a grin, he said, "I came in October. I usually visit, but I think this time, I will be staying for good." We exchanged numbers and addresses, and he stayed in touch with me.

Carl was a typical gentleman. Carl and I became friends during our high school days when he and I met frequently at a taxi stand and talked as we both waited for a taxi. We rode the taxi together, and Carl paid for my ride. My parents were impressed by Carl's gentlemanliness. However, if you knew my parents, especially my father, you would know that it would take a running bull to change his ideas and feelings about his daughters' relationships with male friends. My father felt that our studies mattered more than talking and spending time with boyfriends. When our boyfriends did visit, my father would sometimes interrupt our conversations with them, to our embarrassment. He would say the craziest things like, "Hello, I don't want any panorama in here." He was continually suspicious of our intentions and concluded that it was unusual for two people to simply sit and talk.

But Carl was a strategist. He would make a point to visit me at my parents' home on major holidays, when love and joy abounded everywhere, when strangers and distant relatives were welcomed in our home. Carl never telephoned me before he came to visit, but somehow, I knew when to expect him.

When he visited me, my parents always welcomed him. My mother would always say, "Carl, yuh want some cake and some sweetbread?"

He would always reply, "Thanks, Mrs. Moses." Carl was never shy when it came to eating black cake and sweetbread. Carl loved black cake and sweetbread both then and now. Recently, he has cut back on sweets as that might increase his risk of getting diabetes.

I remember the questions that flooded my head when I was in Trinidad: *Whom would I marry? Which young man would fit my profile?* I was thinking of having a family someday if the Lord willed. I knew Carl and I would have joy in our lives, but we had no idea of the difficulties that lay ahead.

4 Attending College

I obtained an associate degree from a two-year business school in Trinidad and that helped me secure admission to a major university in Boston; all I needed was two and a half years to fulfill the requirements for a bachelor's degree. I was surrounded by positive people at the residence who encouraged me to pursue my dream. One of the women from the residence invited me to dinner at the home of one of her relatives and surprised me with a gift of $300 toward my college education. I was grateful.

When I was accepted to the university, I was so happy that I could not hold back the tears that rolled down my cheeks. The question I faced was, "How would I be able to attend this major college without adequate funds?" After meeting with financial aid personnel and learning that I would receive school loans and a work-study package, I was at ease.

College was challenging, with homework assignments, quizzes, midterms, and final examinations. In 600-person auditoriums, I was lost if I did not take good notes, so if I missed any portion of a lecture, after class, I would compare notes with another student. I lived and worked on campus, working ten hours a week at the business office to assist me with my daily expenses.

During holidays such as Thanksgiving, international students like me were transferred to a dormitory further away from the main campus. That posed additional problems for me, since there were no cafeteria services, no restaurants nearby at the time, and I did not have a car to access reataurants. I was hungry and lonely. On Thanksgiving Day, I walked the streets near the confines of the dormitory in search of restaurants, but I could find very few—only variety stores serving small sandwiches, snacks, and soft drinks. In desperation, I bought a sandwich, a bag of chips, and a Pepsi and returned to my room. Memories of my first day in America surfaced. However, I made it through Thanksgiving Day.

I had no one to turn to except for God, who continually reassured me that I was not alone, that He was with me, and that He would take care of all of my needs. I depended on Him.

In the days, weeks, months, and years following, I was determined to study hard, maintain good grades, and graduate with my Bachelor of Science degree. I was always in the library catching up and studying for midterms and final examinations. On one occasion, while studying for a midterm, I stayed up with fellow students till mid-morning. When I entered the classroom, I knew I could not sit for the examination. I had a throbbing headache and asked the professor for a make-up examination. I was under pressure, particularly during my first semester. The Dean of the School of Management explained that my transfer was dependent on my first semester grade average. I believed him and made the Dean's List. The workload in college continued to be overwhelming, but I knew I had to persevere, so I prayed to God for strength.

5 Getting Married, Celebrating Our Anniversary, and Carl's Birthday

Six months before my college graduation on February 20, 1971, Carl and I were married at a small Roman Catholic church in Boston before a small gathering of friends and relatives. I wore a white satin gown with a pearl necklace and matching earrings. Carl rented a black tuxedo and wore a black bow tie. Our two bridesmaids wore bottle-green velvet dresses. I was lucky to find a beautiful gown at a reasonable price, because neither of us could afford anything luxurious. Neither Carl's parents nor my parents were able to attend our wedding, but we had support from a great mix of friends and family. For our honeymoon, we spent two nights at a local hotel, since I was attending college and we could not afford an elaborate vacation.

Twenty-five years later, we were celebrating our wedding anniversary among family and close friends. Fifty people were in attendance, including our children, Tony, Monique, and Jo-An; my youngest sister, her husband, and their children; and Carl's brother, sister, and niece. Everyone was happy, rejoicing, and really celebrating with us. Our church co-pastors officiated at the service, where we renewed our vows and rededicated our lives. Our reception was held in the basement of our church. As we walked down the aisle, my very good friend waved a scarf at me, and said, "Go, girl." In the basement, my friends decorated the poles, giving them the appearance of large palm trees in the middle of an island. The walls were covered with pictures of Carl and me on our wedding day.

We remembered our younger daughter, Jo-An, on that anniversary day. She wore a floral dress with rose petals against a black background. Her hairstyle, which was dropped curls, was beaming in the light, and everyone could see them from a distance. Although Jo-An was shy, she managed to stand up and make a toast in front of family and friends. Monique wore a black, sleeveless dress and wore her hair in an up-do. With a radiant smile, she got up and said a few words to the audience. Our son Tony wore a black suit and white shirt and acted gentlemanly as he shook hands with relatives and friends. I was really proud of our children. Reese did not make it for our twenty-fifth anniversary celebration.

My husband Carl wore a beige suit, a beige tie, and a white shirt. I wore an off-white, knee-length wool suit, with a matching jacket that was beaded on the front, fitted, with a length just about two inches past my waistline. I found a pair of earrings resembling the pearls on my jacket. Our daughters and I each carried a bouquet of white roses, while my husband and son each wore a white rose boutonnière.

My youngest sister prepared various dishes for the event: curry chicken, barbeque chicken, rice and peas, Spanish rice, and barbeque ribs which everyone enjoyed. Several family and friends made comments concerning both Carl and me, funny at times and, at other times, a bit embarrassing, but we got through them. We even had a photographer, who took pictures during the entire event. It was a day to remember!

We often celebrated our wedding anniversary with two nights in a local hotel where we had fun participating in the hotel's buffet breakfast and going to dinner.

On October 5, 2002, I decided to give Carl a surprise birthday party. We went to our usual local hotel, so he did not suspect anything. I purchased a burgundy shirt for him, and I wore a burgundy blouse to match his shirt. As I was ironing Carl's jacket, I noticed that one button was missing as well as the vest. I realized that he had picked out the wrong jacket from the closet. We could not return home because family members were at our house getting ready for the party. Luckily, the jacket was similar in color to the pants. The iron also left two spots on my shiny burgundy blouse. Carl kept telling me, "You worry too much. No one will see the spot. It is at night, and you will be sitting down to eat." I called every store in town to get another blouse, but every store was out of my size. However, after I put on the blouse, the spots were not obvious. Carl's new shoes were uncomfortable, so we returned them and secured another pair.

I told Carl that I had arranged to have dinner at a local hotel. When I got to the hotel where we were celebrating his birthday, I called our daughter Monique. "How is Jo-An?" I asked. This question was not a strange one, since Monique was caring for Jo-An so we could spend our anniversary together. I later stated, "Don't forget to cover her head." Usually this meant covering her head at night so her hairdo would stay in place. The two questions were codes that we had planned ahead of time, and they meant, "Carl and I are approaching the Madison room of the Sheraton Hotel; cover the sign on the outside door."

When we entered the hotel room, everyone greeted Carl with a shout, "Surprise!!"

Carl was totally surprised! He gave Jo-An his jacket because she was cold. Carl was not bothered by the fact that he was without a jacket. The music was a combination of oldies, some newer songs, and some songs for the young people in our midst. We danced and danced; we really enjoyed the night. We were not the only ones enjoying ourselves, for when I turned, I saw everyone smiling as they danced to the oldies with their husbands.

We returned to the hotel that night. I was glad that everything had worked out well. Carl was still surprised. Next morning, we had a wonderful breakfast with immediate and extended family members, some of whom had come from out of town for the event.

6 Celebrating Birthdays, Christenings, and Holidays

Tony, our first child, Reese, our second, and Monique, our third, were all born in the seventies followed by Jo-An, who was born in the mid-eighties. We were happy to have two sons and two daughters. Life was enjoyable.

My extended family, mother, father, and two sisters came to Boston in 1972, so Carl and I had a community to fall back on. When our children were born, my mother provided the needed daycare services for us for a period of time. During the period of our children's births, my four sisters and brother were also having children, so we had lots of christening and birthday parties to attend. We celebrated christening and birthday parties to commemorate our children's births, God's gifts to us. At four to six weeks after each birth, we had a christening ceremony for our new baby, which we celebrated in a local church before family, friends, and godparents. The godparents stood with us at the altar, and one of them held our child. The minister recited prayers and charged the godparents and parents to bring up the child in the ways of the Lord. The ceremony ended when he blessed the child. It was typical for families to take pictures of the ceremony. After the ceremony, a celebration would follow at our home. Food and drink included pelau, macaroni pie, potato salad, roti, black cake (which resembled a wedding cake), and fruit punch.

Extended family and friends frequented our home for our children's birthday parties. Tony and Reese's birthdays were one week apart, so we held a party for both boys. Our sons' parties were simpler than our daughters'. They invited their friends, ate, talked, and laughed, and that was the end of it. There were never sleepovers, and that was a relief. As our sons got older, we decided to install a basketball hoop outside to keep them busy—wrong move! The boys from the neighborhood lived at our home after that. My home office, situated at the rear of the house, was home to the noise of, "Yes! Yes!" or "I told you I would win!" signifying affirmations of victory. I lived

19

through every exclamation, glad at times to listen to the constant bursts of laughter and joy and the trotting of the feet that was indicative of the game. As I sat there listening, I could not help but remember my life, smothered with so much structure that I did not have opportunities to have fun, so although the noise disturbed me until I had no peace, when I looked at their faces beaming with laughter and joy, I could not say, "I think it's time for you boys to end the game."

The party for our younger daughter, Jo-An, was simple. She had sleep-overs every year except for one occasion, when her party was at Chuck E. Cheese. She would invite the same four girls yearly, her two cousins and two friends. For entertainment, she always had "pin the donkey" and musical chairs.

Our older daughter's party could be a sleepover, a cookout, or a pool party. Monique loved variety. Our home turned into a playground when there was a sleepover. The children played with water balloons on hardwood floors, and we adults stood there, doing nothing until the hardwood floors got slippery and it was time for parental intervention.

"Girls, it is time to stop the water balloons now. You might fall and hurt yourselves."

"Okay."

When it was time for the girls to go to bed, Carl and I would quietly retreat to bed, open-eyed, hoping to hear snoring. Instead, we would hear a never-ending rumble as the girls indulged in pillow fights and endless chattering and laughter. On one occasion, one child cried all night because she had forgotten to bring her security blanket.

"I want my security blanket! I want my security blanket!" she cried.

"Well, sweetheart, your mother forgot to bring it, but I can give you another blanket," I said.

"No, I want my security blanket!"

No blanket in the world could substitute for her security blanket, so I played the role of mother, hugging and consoling her.

When we held the party at Burger King, it was not as much fun as a sleepover, but I did not have to clean up. Unfortunately, Monique hurt herself on the swings outside! We just could not win. Since Monique's birthday fell on Memorial Day, and as she grew older, she opted to have cookouts at our home. As parents, we felt no obligation to have birthday parties for our adult children, but we loved the idea of getting together with family and friends to share, laugh, and enjoy one another.

While the May cookouts continued to be lots of fun, I was always completely exhausted from the enormous amount of food preparation, cleaning, and rearranging that I did in preparation for them. The main course was always pelau (rice and peas with chicken), curry and barbeque chicken, and potato salad. I would do all of the shopping, but Carl did all of the last-minute shopping for items such as ice, candles, paper plates, cups, forks, knives, sodas, and other miscellaneous items. Carl would also barbecue although he did not enjoy doing it. Our friends would arrive early to talk and share, while extended family and others would arrive much later. Our daughter Monique entertained her cousins as late as 10 p.m. I never knew when the party ended, for I would usually retreat to bed about 9 p.m.

Christmas, New Year's Eve, and Easter were festive times in Trinidad, and we continued to enjoy the tradition and, most of all, to thank God for all that He had done and was still doing in our lives. Christmas was a time of joy and excitement as family members enjoyed the traditional: visit everyone, eat, drink, laugh, and be joyous. At Christmas in Trinidad, we opened our doors to receive people dressed in red singing Christmas carols. The songs of Christmas resonated in our hearts, leaving us with peace and joy. Songs included "Joy to the World," which spoke about the coming of the Lord, the Savior of the world, who came to this earth to identify with and make a way for us. New Year's Day was meaningful, the beginning of a new year. God had kept us safe through the past year. Easter symbolized the resurrection, a time to enjoy the hope that Christ afforded us through His death and resurrection. As we remembered our tradition, we prepared our homes and invited our families and friends to celebrate with us and they reciprocated by inviting us to their homes. We prepared traditional West Indian meals and drinks as a reminder of the island from which we came and Whom we served, our Lord and Savior, Jesus Christ. We celebrated that joy with each other, embracing each other and showing our love for one another.

7 Our Children's Growing-Up Years

When our children were much younger, I always maintained a flexible lifestyle: I taught at a community college three days per week and operated a home-based consulting business. Carl was the breadwinner, working full-time and sometimes part-time to supplement our family's income. I did not bring in a whole lot of money, but my schedule allowed me to take our children to their medical and dental appointments and to spend quality time with them without feeling stressed. I loved to surprise them by dropping in during their classes to see how they were doing, to bring cupcakes to school on their birthdays, to drive them home from school on occasion, and to attend school plays, swim meets, and basketball games.

Tony, Reese, and Monique were getting older, entering middle school, changing, and becoming more independent. Monique participated in so many sports that she had difficulty keeping up with her homework. She was having the time of her life. Reese was doing well, particularly in French, English, and his extracurricular activities like music, basketball, and swimming. However, he had a temper with which to contend. Tony was doing well in the earlier grades but sometimes forgot to keep up with his homework. Carl and I visited our children's schools for teachers' conferences or to speak with teachers frequently.

Those were challenging years for me. Carl gave the children and me the support that we needed: driving and accompanying me to parent-teacher meetings and swim meets in the dark, dreary hours during winter season, and picking up our daughter Monique from cheerleading, basketball, or track practice.

Before we ever thought of having cookouts, my husband Carl and I drove up to Reese's school on Memorial Day and actually marched in the school band as Reese played the drums. Reese had an outgoing personality and could charm the dullest person. He excelled in everything he did. He played the guitar and drums, swam, and participated in basketball. In the

1980s, we had occasion to witness his First Communion at his local Roman Catholic school. Reese, now about six feet tall, was dressed in a white suit. Anyone could see his good-looking, dimpled face and convincing smile a mile away. He was stubborn at times. I remember that when he was fifteen, Carl and I drove him to a swim meet, and he refused to swim.

"Go in the water, Reese," I said. "You are not going to waste our time here."

After several promptings, he angrily jumped into the water but did not swim his best.

He came out saying, "I told you I didn't want to swim, but you guys kept forcing me to do it!"

When Reese was sixteen, he begged me once to let him drive my car.

"Mammy, I am not going far; you can trust me."

I replied, "No, you are not driving my car, and that's that!"

My response did not stop him. Reese waited until I was asleep to use my car. The next morning, I awoke to find that my car had been in an accident and needed repairs. I was in tears knowing that I had purchased that used car not long ago and had to decide to either junk it or spend a lot of money repairing it. I chose to repair the car, which, unfortunately, cost the same as the purchase price of the car.

We visited Monique's school on occasion to listen to her play the trumpet or to watch her participate in a play. Monique was the third child but the first girl, so she had to fend for herself and try to be as unique as possible. At one point, she played GI Joe with her brothers. When she realized that she was not part of their team, she networked with friends and participated in swimming competitions, track, and basketball tournaments. She stayed over at friends' homes since her high school was far away.

Monique was not as tall as her sister and her brothers. She was of medium height but had a petite body that was strong. Incredibly beautiful and photogenic, Monique enjoyed herself wherever she went. She was always the joy of any party; her face always looked radiant because of her beautiful smile. She knew how to laugh and bring joy wherever she went. I remember one shopping day when Monique was just about six years old that we could not find her in the Macy's Department Store basement (then Jordan Marsh Department Store). I was shopping for our sons' clothing, and Monique found an opportunity to hide under racks of clothes. She informed me later that she made believe the clothes which surrounded her were a forest filled with trees. She came out of hiding to look for us, started crying, and, when she could not find us, went back to her hiding place.

Tony, our oldest son, was quiet and shy but was not quiet when it came to playing the piano. We loved to hear him play "The Entertainer" at his piano recitals. He was dark and tall, with a slim build and handsome features. He was sociable, and well mannered, and did very well at swim meets. He was the most obedient and respectful child of them all. He never talked back or disobeyed. I remember that when we would speak to him sternly about an issue, he would remain quiet and composed and look intently at us with his bright brown eyes. All three children were great at swimming, so they kept us quite busy with swim meets at different places and at different times.

Everyone remembers me pushing Jo-An in her stroller. Jo-An attended a family daycare followed by a group daycare, which allowed me to maintain my teaching job three days per week. Jo-An was an amazingly easy baby to care for. Because of the surgery I had when she was three months old, I could not continue to nurse her, so she missed the close nurturing that our other children received. As a result, she was always clinging to me.

As Jo-An grew into a child of three, four, five years old, with large black eyes, olive skin, and a peaceful demeanor, she was still the shy, sweet little girl who did not make a fuss about anything but just looked on. She continued to be with me at all times and under all circumstances. She enjoyed dancing classes at a local dancing school when she was five or six years old. She just had the figure for dancing, I thought, with her tall, slim figure, long legs, and pointed toes. She loved getting her face made up, too, with lipstick and eye shadow, getting her nails done, and getting her hair pulled back into a bun.

As beautiful as our children were, we were constantly working hard to get them to understand the need to take responsibility for cleaning their rooms and helping in the kitchen and in the yard.

We always heard from Monique: "Mammy, we are the only ones who do not go downtown alone or go to a friend's house after school."

We were adamant about her coming straight home after school.

"I do not care what other people do. We want to know where you are at all times, and your place is at home. You have homework and chores to do as well."

She often stayed in her room and slept while leaving the television on. Oh, how angry that behavior made me feel; the electric bill was increasing. *"Does this girl understand what it means to turn off the lights?"* I thought to myself.

Reese was a constant challenge. He did not want anyone to talk to him. Often when I came home from work, he would be leaving so he would not have to hear what I had to say.

"Reese, did you clean your room!? I am not going to stand for any nonsense."

"Yes, Mammy."

Tony was quiet, and I had to remind him constantly: "Tony, did you do your weekly chores?"

He would quietly respond, "I know, I know, Mammy. I'll do them later."

As Tony, Reese, and Monique grew in stature and were about to go to college, it began to get more difficult to pin them down to any task.

They were simply normal teenagers with their own agendas.

8 Family Vacations

My dearest friend from the residence was kind enough to make her family cottage available to us, so in August 1986, our entire family traveled to Nova Scotia, Canada. Jo-An was almost 3 years old then, Monique 9, Reese 12, and Tony 14. Jo-An was walking, running, talking, so it was easier for us all.

Our station wagon, which we called our "green machine," was old and rusty. When we started packing our luggage and putting the bicycles on the bicycle rack, I was certain that our car would not make it to Maine. I was nervous the entire time, particularly because we had only enough time to drive there and catch the boat. Carl drove our old station wagon to Portland, Maine, and at approximately 9 p.m., we boarded the *Scotia Prince* with our four children. I knew that going on a trip of that nature, with the entire family, would be a handful, but since I had never gone on a boat ride for such a long distance, I thought it would be exciting. I could not wait to go.

The cabins on the boat were adequate, with double beds and room enough for our family. This was new. Different. Although I experienced seasickness, the journey to and from Nova Scotia for me was not bad because I slept throughout the ride. On our way to Nova Scotia, I attempted to eat a salad, not knowing it was a lobster salad. For a moment after eating the salad, I thought I would faint because of my allergic reaction to shellfish, but I managed to stay strong. The children enjoyed the games on the boat.

While Carl was driving through Nova Scotia in search of my friend's family cottage, our daughter Monique needed to use the bathroom. We knocked at someone's door. A woman came to the door, and we politely asked, "Ma'am, can we please use your bathroom? Our daughter needs to go badly." Surprisingly, the owner opened her door, invited us in, and said, "Certainly, come right in. I will show you to the bathroom."

"Thank you so much. You are so kind," I said.

"You seem to have come a long way."

"Yes, we traveled from Boston, took the *Scotia Prince* from Portland, Maine, and have a distance to go yet before we come to our friend's family cottage." She told us the unique spots to visit and wished us well on our vacation.

We arrived at my friend's family cottage. My family and I remembered the cottage after twenty-two years as one which sat on a hill overlooking a pond and the ocean. It was a three-bedroom suite with bunk beds and a master bedroom, full bath, kitchen, living room, and dining room. The appliances were practically new, the furniture wooden, sturdy, and in exceptionally good condition. The house included a veranda furnished with white chairs and overlooking a garden filled with beautiful flowers that brought a feeling of relaxation, which compensated for the darkness that we experienced inside because of the all-wood furniture. Sitting on the veranda, with rays of sunshine coming through the windows, the beauty of the brightly colored flowers and the friendliness of the people, I pictured myself in Trinidad.

A wooded path from the backyard led to a pond and a few yards beyond was the ocean where the family went daily. We walked into the water up to our waists; the water was warm from the constant sun and clear from the blue skies arching over it, so clear that we could see our reflections. At times, Jo-An and I would stay at the pond area, or I would be involved in teaching her to ride her tricycle.

When we arrived in Nova Scotia, our boys, Tony and Reese, quickly took their bikes off the bicycle rack and toured the neighborhood! Our daughter Monique and my husband, Carl, quickly located the ocean and had a quick swim. They complained often of the bites they got in the water and could not understand what was biting them because the water was so clear! Monique found a friend, and, together, they searched for frogs and grasshoppers, which Monique thought of taking home.

Monique kept coming to me and shouting, "Mammy, my friend and I searched and found frogs. The frogs are different in these parts. They look smaller! I found a grasshopper! Look, I am going to put it in a jar and take it home. Do you think it will live until we get home?"

"I do not think so, Monique. The grasshopper needs air, just like we do."

Jo-An was fascinated with butterflies.

"Mammy, look—a butterfly."

"Jo-An, we have butterflies in Trinidad. Do you remember seeing them? You were probably too young to remember."

Just then, our sons came rushing in. "Mammy, we had fun! This place is so quiet and peaceful. It reminds me of Trinidad. I like the people too."

"Where did you guys go?"

"We rode all around the neighborhood. We got too far and decided to return before we lost our way. It was fun!"

28

Carl and I reviewed the situation. It would cost a lot of money to take our children out to eat three times per day, so Carl opted to buy groceries, and, unfortunately, I agreed to cook at the cottage.

"Okay, Carl, as much as I want to have a vacation, I give up—I will cook simple meals. Will you help me clean?"

"Whatever."

"That's not an answer."

"I will. I will. Just enjoy yourself and stop worrying."

While we were there, we visited a lighthouse and small shops, and we took walks. We prepared meals at the cottage. Carl, the children, and I had a good time. As I reflect now, I don't remember ever having had a better time. Our entire family was together, and everything was beautiful.

Vacations with our children also included family camping in Maine and short trips to the Cape, and an occasional trip to Trinidad. Carl accompanied us when he was not busy at work. He preferred vacations on the island of Trinidad with extended family members and, on occasion, with our sons and daughter. International travel for six people, for me, was too complex and costly. I loved the simplicity of our Maine and Cape vacations, the opportunity to leave house duties behind, to enjoy myself, and to bond with our family without traveling too far. I hated flying!

Camping in Maine was rugged, with bathrooms and showers centrally located, making it difficult during the night when my children and I needed to use the bathroom. However, I loved family camping because it was affordable and included breakfast, lunch, and dinner. Staff activities with the children in the morning and at night allowed me to have time for group activities with other adults or simply afforded me time to rest or go to the movies. After lunch, our children and I spent quality time at the beach, amusement parks, and shopping with camp staff.

In July 1983, I was reminiscing about the beauty of Maine amid the pain that I was experiencing from swollen legs, for I was in my seventh month of pregnancy with our daughter Jo-An. I knew that, even with my discomfort, I was prepared to make the best of our vacation, remaining strong for our children, who depended on me to show them a good time. While thinking of how I could manage alone with our three children, I heard the camp counselor call for them to go to their respective groups. *"Oh, what a great feeling,"* I thought. *"The children will stay busy making various crafts for a whole morning, and I can attend an adult Bible study or have quiet time."* In the afternoon, I took the children to the beach.

As our children got older, we stayed in motels in Maine, which afforded us greater amenities, such as a bathroom in our rooms, a small refrigerator to store milk and juice, an inside swimming pool, a sauna, and a whirlpool. For breakfast, we ate in at times and had lunch and dinner at seafood and fast-food restaurants. We had fun bowling and shopping. Whenever we were in Maine, we visited the Maine camp and took a short tour of the facility and reminisced about the times we spent there.

In July of 2023, I felt the need to return to the Maine camp we had so often frequented, so I invited Reese and his son and Monique and her three children to accompany me. We stayed at a lodge on the Maine campgrounds where we occupied four bedrooms and had access to three bathrooms and a living room. Each room had two twin beds with enough space for all of us. We ate in, the children played games and took naps, and we walked to the beach and did some shopping on our way back to Massachusetts. We reminisced about the great times we had in Maine when our adult children were kids. While we were there, our grandchildren visited the recreational building where our children sang decades ago and pretended to sing songs with the mic before a crowd of people. It was so much fun!

Although we stayed in a hotel and had fun swimming in the hotel pool and shopping on the Cape, we did not have as much fun as we did in Maine. At some point, I decided that I would take only our daughters on future vacations to Maine or the Cape, while my husband would take our sons with him on his vacations to Trinidad.

Our daughters, Monique and Jo-An, accompanied me on my trip to Trinidad in January 1995. We nearly missed the flight from Miami Airport because of the time it took for us to change to another plane. Our worst nightmare on our arrival in Trinidad was finding out that our luggage was missing, and we would have to wait for at least two days to retrieve them. That thought was unnerving.

We spent most of our ten-day trip visiting and having dinner with relatives and friends, having picnics on the beaches and at Maracas Waterfalls while enjoying the birds and the beautiful butterflies, visiting Point-a-Pierre Wild Forest Museum, eating out at Chinese and other restaurants, touring the oil fields, and attending church services at different venues. It was just wonderful to simply walk in the blazing hot sun.

In my growing up years in Trinidad, I did not have as much fun. My parents had encouraged me to work extremely hard in school and to be diligent regarding my spiritual life. I missed the opportunity to learn and enjoy mountain climbing and was not sure that I could climb a mountain. When my children asked me to climb a mountain, I said, "I cannot climb all the way up there. Are you kidding?"

"Mammy, you can do it. Do not look at the height; just put your feet in each cleft. You can do it," they told me.

"Okay, I am going to do this. I am going to overcome this hurdle. I have made up my mind," I thought to myself.

And so, step by step, I walked up and up, higher and higher. I could not believe that I had accomplished what I had set out to do. It was so beautiful to sit and have a picnic lunch and view the waterfalls. What I liked the most was the sight of a beautiful butterfly, which landed right before me with colors of bright splendor. It was not that I had never seen a butterfly, but I had never had the time to pay attention to the beauty and the array of colors it contained.

As I reminisced about my time in Trinidad, I could not help but praise God for His greatness and pray concerning my loneliness and what I had communicated with God about on that summer day in July 1983, pregnant with Jo-An.

9 Taking Day Trips with Our Children

Day trips included shopping trips, medical appointments, church, and mini outings. Since my husband, Carl, worked full-time and part-time on the weekends, when it was time to purchase school clothes, I took all four children to the store. I allotted $150 to each child, and each picked out his or her clothes, except for Jo-An, who was much younger. Shopping days were fun but a bit overwhelming—I could have used another hand. While our sons picked out their clothes, I would help the girls. After shopping, we always sat down to eat. When it was time to fetch the car from the parking lot, I just could not remember where I had parked, so I would walk up and down the parking lot trying to find my car.

For medical appointments, I arranged appointments for our sons on one day and for our daughters on another. We always had a meal in the hospital cafeteria before heading home.

Church was much easier. We attended a Baptist church conveniently located one block from our home. This church was large, with brightly colored stained-glass windows so we could see the sun rays during service. The church had the most unique set up for baptism right there behind the pulpit. There was a stained-glass window with a picture of Jesus beckoning one to come and be baptized. I always took a bag of eatables and activities for the younger ones and had enough to give to another child whose mother was having a hard time. Our children loved the church since they participated in children's church and Sunday school classes, had occasions to sing before the church, interacted with their childhood friends, and particularly enjoyed the food that they served in the fellowship hall following the service.

Mini outings included visits to local zoos and parks, the library, and annual day trips to Martha's Vineyard. On the weekends when Carl was not working, he took us to local and out-of-state parks and beaches such as Nantasket Beach, Houghton's Pond, Canobie Lake, and others. He drove us to our children's swim meets, amusement parks, school plays, basketball tournaments, and musicals. He helped organize the children for their swimming tournaments and for picnics at parks or at beaches, swam with the children, or took them bike riding up and down hills. Riding up and down hills was difficult for me; I just could not do that!

I looked forward to our annual day trip to Martha's Vineyard. I would drive to Woods Hole, park our car, and take a ferryboat over to the island. Our sons would take their bikes so they could ride and keep busy. Our daughter Monique would walk with me while I would push Jo-An in her stroller and view small shops. We would be mindful of the time but always stayed for the entire day, returning to Woods Hole by the last ferryboat. We always had a splendid time.

I used every opportunity to take our children out so that I could have fun at the same time. The Fourth of July was our biggest hit. Carl did not like classical music, but I did, so I thought: *"Who can I think of to accompany me to hear the Boston Pops?"* That was easy. *"Just take our children,"* I thought, and so I did.

I took all four children and loaded their bikes into our car. I got there early in the afternoon and foolishly parked my car in a no-parking zone. The children rode over the BU Bridge while I pushed Jo-An in her stroller. They were excited! Since it was early, the children rode their bikes in the open space in front of the Hatch Shell, but as people began to assemble and sit on the grass, there was little space left for them to ride their bikes or spread their blankets. We spent a long time in the park and by late afternoon had consumed all the food we had. Fortunately for us, there were people sitting next to us barbequing, and they shared what little they had with us. There were issues when it was time for our children to go to the bathroom, but we took care of that the best way we could. Later, after listening to and enjoying the Boston Pops and viewing the fireworks, we were ready to head home.

We walked on the bridge amid droves of people, the boys riding their bikes ahead of us. Monique was walking with her bike beside me while I pushed Jo-An in her stroller. It was late, and our goal was to get to our parked car as quickly as possible. We felt relieved as we approached the location of our car, our sons getting there before us. But where was our car? I was sure that I had parked it there! I had even memorized landmarks.

"Mammy, I think our car was towed!" Reese blurted out.

"Let's call the police station," Tony suggested.

What were we to do? We turned around and walked toward a phone booth two or three blocks away and called the nearest police station. My boys, Tony and Reese, were still riding up and down the street while our daughter Monique was sitting on the ground holding her bike.

34

"Your car was towed, ma'am, and you need to pay a $40 fine," the person on the other line told me.

I called Carl immediately, and he decided to pay the fine, pick up the car, and meet us at the 7-Eleven store. While waiting for Carl outside the store, we came into contact with a woman five feet six inches tall, olive in complexion, wearing her hair in a low Afro style, and who was smartly dressed. Her eight-year-old son was walking beside her. She was swaying from side to side as she spoke to me, and her piercing eyes showed signs of desperation. She was frantic, eager to have her problems solved. She was pleading with me to take her child.

"Mem, could you take meh child?" As she said this, she pushed the child to where our children were standing. The child was sobbing uncontrollably. For a moment, I remained stunned and speechless. Then to my utter amazement, she left her son where we were standing on the pavement and proceeded to walk away.

I said, "Ma'am, I cannot take your child. I have to manage my own children. You cannot leave your child here."

She continued to walk away busily, while her son, crying loudly and feeling lost and rejected, ran after his mother and eventually caught up to her. At the time, I empathized with this woman and her child and wished that I could have been more helpful to her.

At that moment, our daughter Monique began to cry and said, "Mammy, let us go home. I am scared. This woman seems crazy!"

Our sons exclaimed, "Mammy, let us get out of here right now!"

What could I do at that moment? I could not talk with this lady, although I wanted to. My children were frightened and upset. I had Jo-An in my arms. I had a full load. We needed to get home. When we did, I felt relieved. We were safe. All I remember was the superb time we had in spite of the inconvenience we experienced.

10 Going on My Getaways

My getaways were the times I retreated to the Cape to be in the presence of God, to hear from Him, and to evaluate myself as a child of God, a wife, and a mother. I needed to seek God, to renew my mind, and to recognize where God was taking me in my life. Carl supported me, taking time from work to care for our children and doing the best he could with household chores.

I visited the Cape at least once per year for a two-day retreat at a local hotel. In recent years, I have gone to a local hotel several times per year for relaxation, to pray for family and others and to be in touch with God. When I got to the hotel room, the first thing I did was go under the covers. Not having to prepare a meal or do dishes and laundry or speak to another adult was comforting. My going under the covers was a symbol of rest and security with God. I could talk to Him in the peace and quietness of my surroundings without interruption, anxiety, or distractions. I would engross myself in prayer, study His Word, listen to His voice, and write in my journal. That time was special to me because at home I did not have time to do those important things; I was diligent in prayer but not disciplined in studying God's Word.

During my retreats, I recorded my love for the Lord and how I needed to change my ways. I expressed my weariness, my brokenness, my anxieties, my fears, and how I needed God to fix things in my life. I continued to bathe myself in God's love and spent quality time with Him, staying up for hours reading and writing. During the morning hours, I walked, and in the evening, I had a delicious meal, sat in the sauna for a bit, and reverted to the covers again.

My getaways also included small breaks that I took to get out of the house. I visited the library on Thursdays or Saturdays to read and write and visited my natural food store to buy nutritional foods. I felt rejuvenated each time I took small breaks.

One weekend in June 1999, my childhood friend invited me to a conference where she was preaching at a small country church in Louisiana. She was staying at the home of one of the women from the church who gladly welcomed me at her home, which was in a private, wooded area owned by this woman and her family.

The morning of the conference, I took a walk to commune with God. I felt the need to completely surrender everything to God—my household, my life, my job, all that I owned. God was showing me how to love others, even when I did not feel loved, and that love was the tool that I needed in my life to overcome barriers and difficulties. God wanted my attention, and He desired my obedience.

The message at the conference later that day was, "Sitting at the Feet of Jesus and Listening." The Gospel of Luke records two sisters Mary and Martha, who were in the company of Jesus. Martha was busy preparing the house, cleaning, and cooking, while Mary was sitting at the feet of Jesus, listening, and receiving from Jesus, learning about Him, and getting to know Him intimately. "But Martha was serving, and she approached Him and said, 'Lord, do you not care that my sister has left me to serve alone? Therefore, tell her to help me'" (Luke 10:40 NKJV).

"And Jesus answered and said to her, 'Martha, Martha, you are worried and troubled about many things. But one thing is needed, and Mary has chosen that good part, which will not be taken away from her'" (Luke 10:41-42 NKJV). Often, we are so busy doing ministry that we forget to sit, hear, and learn what, where, and how Jesus wants us to conduct the ministry that will glorify HIM.

In 2003, I attended a conference in Vermont, and the title of the message was, "Blessed to be a Blessing." It was taken from Hebrews 6 and Mark 5. The speaker summarized her message by saying, "Jesus Christ answers desperate cries, even those of the demonic man who was in bondage and lived in utter loneliness, torment, deeply scarred, and rejected." She continued, "Only Jesus could subdue him. Human eyes could not see the potential in the man of 'The Gadarenes,' but God did. God gave him an 'inheritance of glory, a passion for hearts, a birthing of revival.'" The Lord, the king of glory, reaches and helps us in our darkness and in our loneliness. God heals us when we are at our worst, and He uses the least of us.

11 Graduations

The year 1994 marked a turning point in our lives. Monique graduated from high school that year, applied to a prestigious college and gained acceptance. I remember her high school graduation day; it was bright and sunny. Her ceremony took place outside in the open field. Monique's supporters were her immediate family and her cousins. Her face lit up with radiant smiles as our group cheered, "Go, Monique. Go, Monique." After the ceremony, she received kisses, hugs, and flowers. Monique was happy to see her immediate and extended family who took a lot of pictures with her. She looked radiant and happy! We were proud of her as she moved to another level in her life.

Four years later, in May 1998, she was graduating from college with her Bachelor of Science degree commemorating a great event in her life, as well as in ours. We looked forward to experiencing the joy of seeing a son or a daughter receive a degree from a college. Her ceremony was inside. As they were about to call Monique's name, I avoided the eyes of other spectators and moved closer so I could get to where she was getting her diploma, and yes, I got a good snapshot of her. We were not as wild as we were for her high school graduation, but we were wild. "Hey, hey, hey," we exclaimed as she stood up.

I had taken time to choose a beautiful bouquet of flowers for her. The bouquet included roses and lilies of bright Caribbean colors: yellow, orange, and pink. She had worked hard to graduate from high school and now college. We were proud parents. What great accomplishments! What joy! What freedom! Monique's graduation was delightful. My youngest sister and her husband, nieces, nephews, and one of my friends attended the graduation. My husband Carl accompanied our younger daughter, Jo-An, and came to the graduation later so I could get Monique to her graduation on time. They got lost in the crowd and were unable to find us.

Our oldest son, Tony, was serving as a reservist in the military once per month during the late nineties. He graduated from high school, and applied to and received acceptance to a local college. Tony and his fellow classmates were so happy on their graduation day from high school that they threw off their hats after receiving their diplomas. My mother, Agnes, who came to live in Boston, Carl, Jo-An, and I later took our son out to lunch. My mother had a wonderful time eating out at a restaurant.

Carl and I also attended Tony's college graduation. We were excited for Tony as we screamed, "Go, Tony. Go, Tony." Tony was smiling and incredibly happy. We took him out to eat afterward, and two of his cousins joined us. Tony felt happy that he had accomplished his dream of graduating from college with a bachelor's degree. As with all our adult children, we helped Tony after graduation until he was able to be on his own.

It was great having Monique home again. She was returning home after having been away for four years, was independent, and was not ready to abide by rules and regulations. We co-signed for her first car, agreeing to pay her monthly insurance premiums. She worked and made the install-ment payments. Before long, she was attending graduate school. We sup-ported her in that endeavor because we were interested in her future. She completed her Master of Education degree and graduated in 2000. In 2010, she received her Certificate of Advanced Graduate Study from Simmons certifying her to become a principal. We celebrated with her at Maggiano's Little Italy restaurant in Boston. In 2016, as a wife and mother of three, Monique graduated from Boston College with a Doctor of Education. In her presence was one of the preachers who officiated at her wedding and at her children's christening ceremonies. We had a scrumptious Jamaican dinner after her graduation ceremony.

Jo-An graduated from daycare and kindergarten in her earlier years but did not have a formal high school graduation because she attended special schools because of her disability. However, we celebrated various occasions with Jo-An, including her dance recitals, where she received flowers.

Reese, like Jo-An, did not have a formal graduation ceremony from high school, but we celebrated his musical shows prior to high school where he played the guitar, the clarinet, and the drums. Since my husband Carl completed his course work for his Bachelor of Science and master's degree later in the year, he felt that it was unnecessary to attend each graduation ceremony the following year.

I had the opportunity of graduating six months after my wedding with an undergraduate degree in business. I did not attend the ceremony the following year. Six years later, pregnant with our daughter Monique, I took graduate courses and received a Master's in Business Management. I cele-brated my graduation with my husband and my sisters at a seafood restau-rant in Boston.

In 2004, I graduated from seminary with a Master of Arts degree, with a concentration in women's ministry. That was the best and greatest time of my life. In April of that year, I attended an awards ceremony held at the seminary's main campus in South Hamilton, MA, where I received The Robert J. Lamont Award for Academic Excellence. In the opinion of the faculty, the individual receiving the award was likely to apply his or her beliefs effectively to personal and social problems in the work of the pastorate.

On April 30, 2004, Carl and I attended a banquet at the Sheraton Ferncroft in Danvers, MA, and on May 1, 2004, my immediate family and friends surprised me by attending a banquet hosted by the local seminary in Boston where I attended. They bombarded me with flowers!

On May 6, 2004, the day before my graduation, I cleaned the house thoroughly since our daughter Monique was staying at our home with Jo-An and was taking her to the graduation luncheon. I had forgotten to buy a memory card for my digital camera. I thought I would do so when I arrived at South Hamilton later that night for the graduation church service. However, Carl and I got lost on the way and barely made it in time. I did not know how to erase some pictures and make room for others. I did not plan well. However, I had purchased a small camera for my husband to use to take pictures. He took pictures from far away! The service was remarkable! We heard from two students who gave teary-eyed testimonies. The praise and worship time was awesome!

We arrived at the hotel at approximately 10:30 p.m. I was exhausted and anxious, so I could not sleep. When I was about to fall asleep, my husband was waking up at his usual time of 4:30 a.m. to make his morning tea. I sobbed at the thought that I would not feel rested for my important day.

That morning, we started out on our trip once more. This time, we got there without any difficulty because the day was sunny and bright. I got there in time for the group photo. Following the taking of the photo, we went to a certain building to receive a briefing on the graduation procedures. Carl met me as I was marching in with my fellow students and handed me my makeup bag, which did not contain my cell phone, my glasses, or my camera, which we had accidentally left in the car. My eyes hurt during the graduation ceremony.

After the ceremony, all the graduates marched to another building to obtain their diplomas. All my friends, including Kate, then my daughter-in-law-to-be, took pictures as I left the ceremony. I truly felt loved and appreciated. In the midst of the excitement, I did not think to tell them, and neither did I have a cell phone to let them know, to which building I was headed to collect my diploma, so no one knew where Carl and I were. Carl faithfully remained at the building where the graduation ceremony was held, so he was able to find me when I returned to the building looking for everyone. Luckily, everyone remembered where we were going to have lunch, and we met up there.

When Carl and I got to the restaurant, we walked into the wrong room, where another party was celebrating, and everyone yelled out, "Congratulations! What college did you graduate from?" I told them of the seminary and the location, smiled, and quickly left the room, embarrassed. When we finally got to our room, overlooking the water, our entire party was there, waiting patiently: two of my friends and their husbands, and my immediate family.

Everyone presented me with gifts, which they insisted I open before lunch. Our table included gifts and flowers of different colors— white and red roses, pink, orange, yellow—that added such beauty, such elegance and warmth to the occasion, a sign of everyone's love, care, and willingness to share my important moment with me. Our scrod dinner was delicious. We took pictures inside and outside, capturing the picturesque view of the restaurant overlooking the waters.

12 Celebrating Our Son's and Our Daughter's Special Day

Our son Tony emerged from a quiet young person to a man with purpose. He knew what he wanted and took small, yet steady, steps to achieve his goals. Before starting college, he joined the military in 1994 as a reservist. The experience was tough, but, through it, he learned discipline, structure, and focus. By the time he graduated from college, he had satisfied the requirements of the military and was on his way to achieving other goals. He purchased his first home and waited for the day when he would marry the right person. That day finally came on June 25, 2005, when he married Kate.

Family members on both sides were excited for the couple as we looked forward to their wedding day. The bride's family allotted us seventy-five seats, for which we were thankful. It was difficult deciding who to invite because of the size of our extended family and because everyone wanted to be there, but because it was impossible to please everyone, we concentrated on aunts and husbands and two adult children per household. My friends, dear to us, had witnessed Tony's growth from a small child to an adult and had to be counted. I felt a sense of excitement and fulfillment about the steps that our son had taken.

The bride and her parents planned the wedding, while my husband Carl and I paid for the rehearsal dinner and transportation. The rehearsal was fun and relaxing. We practiced walking down the aisle and joked when we made errors. Following the rehearsal, we had a scrumptious dinner of chicken, fish, and dessert. We viewed an entertaining video of Tony and his wife when they were growing up; it brought back memories when we saw my mother holding Tony as an infant.

Carl and I stayed overnight in a hotel with other wedding guests, including our daughter Monique, who was one of the bridesmaids. Jo-An was unable to attend the wedding because she was ill; a friend stayed at our home to care for her. Feeling nervous on the day of the wedding, I decided to wake up early to put on my makeup and get help from Monique, if necessary.

The limousine driver did his rounds in a timely manner, picking up the bridesmaids, then the ushers, Carl and myself, dropping off the brides-maids and myself at the mother of the bride, Ann's, house, taking the ushers and Carl to the church, and finally taking the bridesmaids and myself to the church.

It was exactly 1 p.m. when we arrived at the church. It was 91 degrees, hot indeed, and the skies were blue. Family and friends were seated in a quaint country church with stained-glass windows, Kate's family's church. No one seemed to bother about the heat as it threatened to smear the made-up faces of family and friends looking on and anxiously waiting for the bride.

The mothers walked in first. Carl accompanied me and her nephew Larry, accompanied Ann while we listened to the song, "You Raise Me Up," by Loveland Graham. Carl was dressed in a black tuxedo, grey vest, and white shirt, while I was dressed in a long, sky-blue satin skirt with a slight tail, and a matching tailored jacket with gold sequins, Chinese color, and half-length sleeves. Ann wore a two-piece, pale pink dress and matching jacket. Larry, like the ushers, wore a black tuxedo, grey vest, and white shirt. As the song, "You and I," by Stevie Wonder was played, the best man, Reese, and the maid of honor, Paula, followed by the bridesmaids and ushers, walked in, then the bride and her father, Nathan.

The bridesmaids wore pale pink chiffon and satin dresses and carried burnt rose flowers and pale pink peonies. The bride wore an ivory, A-line Victorian lace dress with a scalloped, beaded top. Her train was also scal-loped, with beading and lace. Her father wore a black tuxedo, grey vest, and white shirt. Reese was smiling and celebrating his brother's happiness. The colors, the flowers, and the sun beaming through the stained-glass windows made the whole processional breathtaking! The mothers lighted the candles, while the song, "Ave Maria," by Bach/Gounod was played. Aunts recited their assigned Scriptures, and tributes were made to grandmothers. The preacher delivered a well-received message. The bride and groom said their "I dos." Everyone looked happy and was rejoicing. Carl and I were immensely happy! We were commemorating our son's special occasion.

At the reception, my sisters, brother, nieces, nephews, some of Carl's relatives, and his and my friends were all there. Their faces were covered with smiles. We hugged, took pictures, and celebrated together. After a delicious dinner, our son and I danced. I was nervous at first, for I wanted everything to go well on his special day. I remembered stepping on my son's feet in the beginning, but I made up my mind to do the best I could! Then, it was over, and we could enjoy the rest of the evening. I looked over at Tony as he danced with his wife and shook the hands of the many guests and family members who were present. That was the happiest day of his life, and he deserved every minute of it.

When Monique decided on a wedding date, I was on a journey with her accompanying her to get her gown, shoes, and accessories, to select her bridesmaid dresses, flowers for the bride and bridesmaids, and helping her keep appointments for alterations, helping her select a photographer, a videographer, an instrumentalist, and going to see the places we had called as potential venues for her wedding.

One place in Canton, MA, limited us to a Friday wedding which did not work out. We looked at another space in Dover, which included dormitory rooms and bathrooms which seemed adequate for our out-of-town guests as they would be in one place; however, the wedding reception would be held outside under a tent and we would be responsible for lighting, tables and chairs, plates and silverware, and other costs. We kept our appointment at the venue in Cambridge, and unfortunately, the hotel had a blackout, and we were unable to take a tour of the building. We visited a university club overlooking Boston, which hosts weddings, but while it looked great, the oblong room was insufficient for our needs. Alas, Monique found the Marriott Hotel Waterfront, which was ideal for her wedding.

The hotel, overlooking the water, gave a tremendous view, and the wedding coordinator assisted Monique with details associated with the menu, the cake, the seating, the rooms, and the decoration for each table. The hotel was ideal as it had sufficient space for the wedding party to rest upstairs and partake of hors d'oeuvres. My daughter and I were fortunate to sleep overnight at the hotel avoiding the rush to get there in the morning. We had breakfast at the hotel that morning and before getting dressed, spent time with a makeup artist and a beautician. I was excited for Monique and could not wait for the wedding celebration to start. I felt special that day—a day that I will always remember.

The time was approaching for Monique to get in her car and arrive at the church for her wedding service. As she walked down the escalator, I remember the people on the other side were just in awe of how she looked. The bride wore an off-white strapless tapered dress that matched her pearl necklace and earrings. She looked absolutely stunning!

There were four bridesmaids, two junior bridesmaids, and one maid of honor, who were all dressed in lime green dresses holding a bouquet of yellow flowers with a dash of green which contrasted well with their green dresses. The three flower girls were dressed in white and wore green sashes to match the green dresses that the bridesmaids wore.

45

The church service was beautiful. The soloist sang "Ave Maria," the groom's mother and I read Scripture verses, those who were scheduled to read did so, and yes, Monique and her husband got married, had pictures taken, and returned to the hotel for an exceptional reception.

13 Receiving Bundles of Joy

The nights rolled on, and the days progressed, nearing the time of the delivery of Kevin, our first and, so far, our only grandchild, who would be born to Tony and Kate. By June 7th, 2007, I was already receiving calls from my sisters, who already had lots of grandchildren. They could not wait to celebrate with me. Both Tony and Kate had kept me abreast of the progress of the pregnancy, and as I had talked and prayed with Kate on Friday, we had agreed that Kevin was on his way to Mother Earth.

By 11:45 p.m. on Saturday, our son called to tell us that Kate was in labor, and from that moment on, I had difficulty sleeping. I cleaned, did laundry, and, before returning to bed at about 3 a.m., I prayed. By early the next afternoon, about 2 p.m., Kate's contractions had increased, and the baby was getting ready for birth. From 2 p.m. until 5:57 p.m., I was becoming uneasy, sensing that something was taking place. A few minutes after 6:00 p.m., I received a call from our son telling me that Kate had given birth to Kevin.

He said, "Hi, Mammy, I have great news for you. Kevin is here. You have nothing to worry about; you are now a grandmother, and I am a father."

I was overcome with emotion. "What! I will be there in a few minutes," I replied. I did not wait to hear the details but quickly got off the phone, related the information to Carl, and was on my way to the hospital. Carl stayed at home with our daughter Jo-An and visited Kate and Kevin the following day. Kevin was born Sunday, June 9, 2007. He weighed 7 lbs. 9oz., was nineteen inches long, and had his first picture taken with him sucking his thumb.

Our children Reese and Monique met me in the waiting room at 7 p.m. We chatted with Tony for a while about the delivery. Tony was doing well, considering what he had gone through the previous hour. We waited for another hour and forty-five minutes before we were able to go to the room to see Kate and Kevin.

As the three of us approached the room, we spotted a nurse tending to a baby just outside Kate's room. Monique ran toward the baby in the tiny bassinet and excitedly said, "Mammy, he is so cute."

In that instant, the attending nurse rudely said, "I'm sorry; you are going to have to wait outside until we are finished!"

Reese was sleepy from his long day at work, but we encouraged him to stay. We had waited two hours so far, and then waited in the hallway for another half hour, but Kevin was worth the wait. We waited and waited; the half hour wait seemed endless, but it ended. The nurse said smilingly, "You can come in now," and in an instant, we rushed into the room.

I said, "Kate, I am proud of you, girl. I knew you could do it. We are not going to stay too long because we know you had a long and rough day."

She said, "Thanks for your patience, Mother Blake; you heard all the things that Kevin and I went through? Tony, my mother, and I were crying. The baby's shoulder was stuck in the birth canal; I had no strength to push, and Kevin was not breathing when he finally came out. This is another testament to God's goodness, first allowing me to become pregnant, and now, saving our baby's life."

At ten at night, after nineteen hours of labor, Kate still had a beautiful smile on her face. She exhibited courage, strength, and persistence to the end. Tony was ecstatic, smiling, and sending emails and text messages to all his friends. He kept on reminding me, "Mammy, you are a grandmother now, and I am a father."

The next few moments were like finding a jewel in a haystack. First, Monique, with tears running down her cheeks, picked up Kevin and said, "He is so cute!" then offered him to me, then picked him up from my lap, then gave him to Reese.

Reese said, "Nah, I don't want anything to happen to him."

I could see a few drops of tears on Reese's face as Monique told him, "You can do it. This is how you hold a baby. Relax your arms, making sure you give the baby head support." Reese held Kevin for about two or three minutes, looking at him closely and enjoying the moment when uncle and nephew came together.

Then, Monique offered the baby to me. "Mammy, do you want to hold him again?"

"Yes," I replied.

I sat down, holding this bundle of joy. I could not believe that God could send so much joy into my life. I perused his entire body. He had so much hair, and it was curly too. He had the cutest cheeks, the brightest eyes, the most readable lips; his face was olive in color, but his feet and hands were even lighter. Kevin was alert and ready to achieve greatness at all levels. As I viewed this grandchild from top to bottom, I understood what God was telling me again and again—that nothing was impossible with Him, and that Kevin was born with a purpose.

As the days and weeks passed, I had an opportunity to spend hours with Kevin and his parents. It was a joy for me to change his diaper, feed him, hold him, rock him in my arms, and see his piercing, dark brown eyes as they met mine. I am so grateful to God for giving me the gift of being a grandmother. I will cherish this gift as long as I live.

Today, my husband Carl and I are the happy grandparents of six grand-children, including Kevin who turned seventeen and has his driver's license. We have two girls, ages 5 and 14, and four boys, ages 8, 9, 10, and 17. We continue to express joy at the birth of each grandchild, joy to care for them on occasions, joy to be there for their christenings, birthdays, their dance recitals, to spend time with them at the library, seeing them paint a picture, play with Legos, or interact with others.

14 Experiencing Various Emotions

In the previous edition of *Standing on His Promises*, I discussed anxieties, fear, fear of sickness, guilt, anger, and unforgiveness that I experienced. Today, I no longer experience these emotions as my prayer life and my relationship with God deepened. I feel that I can depend on God fully as I understand who He really is. He loves me more than anyone else can. He has a plan and a purpose for my life and that of my family. He shows me that He is in control of every situation that I face and that the battle is not mine but His. He brings me out of every situation, gives me endurance, and helps me to utilize my faith in the midst of my struggles.

In the past, anger was my greatest challenge. I could not get over my anger when someone said something about me or treated me unfairly, but I learned that anger and resentment lead to unforgiveness and unforgiveness was the greatest hurdle for me to overcome. It was difficult for me to forgive someone because I viewed that person as needing to be punished for what the person did. Forgiving that person, I thought, was letting him or her off the hook. What I did not know was that unforgiveness was destroying my relationship with God. What I needed to do was repent and ask God for forgiveness for my unforgiving heart.

The Bible states in Matt. 6:15 that if we do not forgive others their sins, our heavenly father will not forgive us our sins.

15 Having Friends

My husband's friends were his childhood friends from Trinidad who visited him annually for Christmas celebrations or who dropped in from time to time, while my friends included friends I knew from Trinidad, friends from former churches, and from the residence where I stayed when I came to America.

Four of my friends and I were from a former church. We met consistently as a support group for two years to support one another. When we met and discussed our pain, our struggles, and our family issues, we knew that we could count on one another to listen, to comfort, to strengthen, and to encourage. While pregnant with Jo-An, I expressed my struggle with keeping up with housework and the women shared their love and support by painting our living room. One person did a load of laundry, another made me a maternity blouse, another cooked a meal, while another accompanied me to my pregnancy classes, came to the hospital at 4 a.m., and stayed with me during labor and witnessed Jo-An's birth.

We five did not have everything in common. In fact, each person was unique and had different goals and viewpoints, yet we were committed to our friendships. One of the women moved to another state but received visits from two members and some of us met with her when she and her husband came into town. At times, I had the honor of praying with this powerful prayer warrior. The remaining four of us met for breakfast or lunch occasionally, talked about issues in our families, and exchanged presents for Christmas. We attended baby showers, christenings, weddings, wedding anniversaries, cookouts, graduations, and the funeral services of loved ones. Since this writing, another member moved out of state and the three of us spent a wonderful time with her. One of the three remaining members invites me to her home and to events occasionally and has become a close family friend to our entire family.

There were other friends from this former church who came to our cookouts and invited Carl and me to their homes during the summer and Christmas seasons. We were also friends with a couple whose daughter and Jo-An became friends at school and attended each other's birthday parties. It seemed that every time I had car failure after dropping Jo-An off at school, I would get help from this family. The fact that we could support each other in good times and in bad made our friendship strong. When we met at their home, our home, or the YMCA, we supported one another. This friend moved to another state, but we kept in touch.

My dear friend who is my daughter Monique's godmother and I met up occasionally for tea at her home or at a nearby café. She celebrated her birthday one year at a restaurant in Boston and invited Monique and eight of us, some of whom had lived at the residence. She treated us to a lavish tea and a harpist entertained us. We reviewed our past pictures, took new ones, and reminisced about the times we had together. We have not met consistently because of Covid-19 and situations beyond our control. However, we stay connected through email, text, and phone calls and have just begun meeting for tea and lunch.

I met a friend while working at a particular job here in Boston who moved out of state. I attended her wedding and, today, I still stay connected with her. I have friends whom I met at conferences who I visit on occasions. These friends mean so much to me because God's love bonded us together.

I gained friends from churches that I attended, from seminary, from my local YMCA, and from our neighborhood. Some of us formed a prayer group and we met for a season at our home. God chose someone to be my prayer partner; this friend prays for my family daily and I also pray for her family. God put friends in my path for me to bless them and, in turn, for me to receive blessings from them. May God be praised.

16 Remembering My Dad

I n April 1985, while teaching at a community college, I felt an urgent need to visit my ailing dad, whom we referred to as "Daddo."

Daddo encouraged me to be my best. However, he was a disciplinarian who did not give us the freedom that we wanted. Daddo did not allow us to go to parties or have boyfriends as teenagers. He encouraged us to study hard and excel. Daddo did not finish high school because his father, his only living parent at the time, had died when Daddo was a boy. However, Daddo had an excellent vocabulary from extensive reading, and he was knowledgeable in English and mathematics, so he helped us with our homework. He was critical of us when we did not speak proper English and often lost his temper when we did not do well in school but would soften up when he received a good report.

Daddo was articulate and loved speaking at political events in our community. When my dad was not working, he participated in the day-to-day issues surrounding our lives, making sure we did our chores and tending to our other needs. When we girls had arguments, he would help us solve our problems by mediating and by giving us opportunities to voice our opinions. We did not have a voice in other matters, though, for his voice was the final voice, and that was just how things were.

When I was in high school, my dad paid for someone to help my mom do the laundry, starch, and iron all the family clothes. He said to my mom one day, "Agnes, Joan is staying up till the wee morning hours to catch up with her studies. We cannot have her doing all this work. I know you cannot do it either, but we have to find someone to help with the washing and ironing on Saturdays so she can do her homework."

"John, she can't even get up in the morning," my mom replied. "What yuh say goes."

Because of my father's deep concern for my education, his decision to hire someone freed me from excessive housework, and I was able to use my time more effectively. At one time, my father wanted to buy a family car so I could drive to business school. He took driving lessons, but his second lesson proved to be a disaster. He slammed into a tree and gave up the car idea completely. I never knew why he did not have me try to get my license.

When I was preparing to go to America, my dad made me wool pajamas and two-piece suits. He whispered in my ear, "Do not worry about anything. You are going to make something of yourself and make a way for us." I later sponsored my mother and father as permanent residents in America. They lived in Boston in the early seventies but returned to Trinidad when my father became ill.

My father had a great sense of humor, and when our sons were little, he loved to wrestle with them. Reese and Tony would scream, "Ouch, Grandpa, that hurts! Grandpa, you are funny!" My dad would actually bite them while he was wrestling, so he always came out the winner.

In April 1985, I traveled with our daughters, Monique and Jo-An, then eight and two years old, to Trinidad to visit Daddo. Monique pushed the carriage while I carried the carry-on luggage. We literally had to run toward the plane in Miami.

I stood to lose my teaching job when I left Boston to visit my father. I was leaving two months before the close of a final semester, and that made me feel insecure. However, the thought of my father passing before I got a chance to see him or hear his last words was frightening. That gave me the zeal to go. As I made my decision, I remembered that when we had earthquakes in Trinidad, my dad, my mother, and us children would hold each other closely, pray together, and resolve to die together.

As a child, I would always say, "If my father should die, I will go with him." My dad recognized my voice when I arrived and responded with a familiar smile of reassurance that made me feel special. The unsaid words were, "I knew I could count on you to visit me. I am glad you are here." I, too, was thankful that I was there. I knew that I had done the right thing for him and for me.

17 Struggling to Know God's Will

Returning to my immediate family was a relief after Daddo's funeral. I was thankful for how God had guided me through the entire process. I continued to give God thanks for everything: for keeping me under the umbrella of His wings, for loving me, for bringing me out of the miry clay, and for setting my feet on solid ground. I began to thank Him for my circumstances, recognizing that when I was out of control, He was in control of my life; thanking Him that He was making a way out for me, that He was lighting my lamp; and thanking Him for being patient with me during my entire life. I prayed that God would set me apart to minister the gifts of comfort and healing to others.

During my pain and struggle, God continued to fill my heart with joy. I had joy just seeing our children happy. In June 1993, Monique was off to her junior prom dressed in a bottle-green, knee-length dress. She and her friends looked gorgeous in their prom dresses.

By July 1993, however, I was struggling to know God's will for my life. I continued to ask God to teach me to wait on Him, to wash me thoroughly with hyssop, to make my heart as white as snow, to remind me that I am His and that no one can snatch me out of His hands. In my prayers, I told God how much I loved Him and that I was leaving all to follow Him. I discerned that God had a purpose for me, and I began to ask Him to reveal it to me, to guide and give me strength for the battle ahead. I had no idea that I would face battles, and that God was giving me strength to go through impending storms.

18 Remembering My Mother/ Dealing with Her Passing

My mother, Agnes, was slightly heavy, with a rounded face and olive skin. We called her "Mammy." Mammy wore dresses and skirts even at home, and she wore her grey hair in single braids. When she went out, she would pull her hair back into a bun to look elegant. She wore glasses. My mother never worked outside the home, except when she was a seamstress, designing bridal and other clothing for people in the community, but that was long before she had us kids. She also designed all of our clothes, making us beautiful dresses for church, for Easter, or for special occasions.

My mother, although less learned than my father, spoke to teachers on our behalf. She had the smile, the drive, and the energy to speak to people in high places. She always found the words to say. She got us into good schools and part-time jobs when school was out. In our growing up years, we did not have a whole lot, yet we were one of the best-dressed families in the neighborhood, and we ate the most delicious meals. What I remember most was that life had meaning and that my parents instilled in us the need to work hard if we were to reach our potential and achieve our goals.

Mammy was very committed to caring for us, especially when we were ill. As a child, I suffered with asthma, and my healing was a result of my mother's faith in the healing power of God and of her diligent care of me. She would wake up during the night and put hot towels on my chest to ease the pain and to help me breathe easier. She would also give me cod liver oil and vitamins daily to build my immune system.

Mammy was a diligent woman, working in the house, cooking, cleaning, washing, and ironing. For breakfast, Mammy made us fried and roast bakes, cornmeal cereal, sago, and other types of porridges. She also prepared all types of herbal teas from the leaves that she secured from her garden. Mammy made the most scrumptious meals, desserts, and juices. She cooked soups with cornmeal dumplings in them. Every meal came with a side order of vegetables and legumes. On Sundays, in addition to our regular meals,

Mammy cooked macaroni pie or potato salad. During the week, she cooked curried dishes, pelau, and an array of root vegetables including dasheen and eddoes. On the days when Mammy fried or stewed king fish, red fish, and shark, she included a side dish of coo-coo.

My mother and I spoke briefly on the telephone in early December 1994. She wanted me to visit her in Trinidad for the Christmas season. That was not possible since I always spend Christmas with my immediate family. I waited till January 1995 to visit her, not knowing that my mother was on the verge of dying.

During our January visit, Monique, Jo-An, and I stayed at my mother's house, which was located in a small, working-class village, which gave us access to local taxis, buses, churches, mom and pop stores, downtown Port-of-Spain, and surrounding areas. She had renovated our home into a large two-story brick house which did not have the cozy feeling of our old wooden, two-bedroom home with which we were accustomed. The house sat on a hill overlooking the street, which gave it beauty and uniqueness. Wild tropical plants covered the front and side landscape, and mango trees compassed the rear yard. It was easy to secure a mango from the hanging branches of the mango trees laden with mangoes. Also, in the rear of the yard, my mother kept her washing tub and ribbed scrubbing board, used for washing clothes by hand.

On our visit to Trinidad in January 1995, my mother looked very thin and frail. She had no zeal to do the usual: attend church services, go to the market, cook, or eat. She was showing unusual signs.

In April 1995, my youngest sister traveled to Trinidad because my mother had taken a turn for the worse. Her exact condition was not quite clear, but my sister decided to bring her to Boston for treatment. My mother had known she was extremely ill and had wanted me to spend Christmas with her. When I visited her in January, I had been focused on my children and myself, wanting to have a good time, not realizing that my mother was ill. Once I discovered the extent of her illness, I felt guilty for my failure to spend time with her in a meaningful way.

In May 1995, she was admitted to a local hospital in Boston and was diagnosed with cancer and had just a few months to live. We were going to lose our mother. I was working at home, so at times I joined my youngest sister and her husband, who made daily visits to the hospital to be at my mother's bedside. I knew that my mother was in constant pain, and that could explain her lack of expression. Her watery eyes seemed to stare into oblivion, not focusing on the people around her but knowing they were there. She ate when I fed her, and I felt satisfied about that. She never acknowledged the prayers that I said on her behalf. She showed signs of depression and disappointment when her attending physician informed her of the seriousness of her illness and that she had only a short time to live. To this day, I am not sure whether my mother had prepared herself to meet her Maker. But, of course, who am I to judge her?

In June 1995, my youngest sister asked that my mother be moved to her home. There, I painfully watched my mother deteriorate as her time approached. My other sisters and I took turns caring for her, but the bulk of the responsibility remained with my sister and her husband, who were constantly at my mother's bedside, bathing her, changing her, feeding her, and providing for her every need.

My mother's passing was sudden and frightening for all of us, especially for my youngest sister. She called me in the middle of the night when my mother died in July 1995.

"Joan, Mammy just died. I have never experienced this, so I am a little frightened. However, Mammy looks the prettiest she has ever been."

She did look peaceful when she died. Death had never come so close to our doors (except for when our father had passed in November of 1992), so we were both nervous, teeth chattering, shivering, and speechless. After calling a funeral home to fetch the body, my sister and I had a good night's sleep and began the funeral arrangements the following day; the burial took place in Trinidad during the month of August.

Although we made many of the arrangements in Boston, we were still running around making last-minute plans in Trinidad. The funeral service was held at a Roman Catholic cathedral among some of my mother's closest friends and only a fraction of her relatives. The service was short and did not have the kind of family involvement that one gets here in the United States.

After the burial, friends and family members gathered nightly to pray, support, and comfort one other. Families shared by bringing food and drink. I felt strange taking a leadership role, a role that my mother previously had: cooking, making the necessary preparations, and welcoming guests as they came by. Having left Trinidad many years ago, I had to reintroduce myself to a few relatives. I faced challenges during this period and wished I were at home, but God strengthened me during the process.

19 Taking a New Job New Challenges

I n January 1996, my husband, Carl, informed me that a government agency had openings for full-time auditors and that I stood a good chance of obtaining one of the positions advertised in the local paper. I prepared a functional resume describing my experiences. I wanted the resume to be printed on off-white paper stock matching the envelope, but after missing the application deadline, I decided to take the chance and mail it as it was. What did I have to lose? I sought career counseling to help me with the interviewing process. Amazingly, I received a call for both an initial and follow-up interview and was offered a position as a full-time tax auditor.

My career was off to a good start when God provided for me in January 1996. I was extremely happy but also a bit anxious. I received my initial six-month training under an experienced auditor before being on my own. With laptop in hand and professionally dressed, I went from company to company and performed sales and use tax audits. I liked the fact that I was out of the office and managed my own caseload. I was really getting a handle on my job and beginning to like it a lot when my life began to turn again for the worse.

Jo-An, our youngest, twelve and a half years old at the time, was experiencing anxiety at school and was losing focus. She preferred to read at recess rather than make friends. However, she always managed to have at least one or two friends. She was well read and had a wide vocabulary; she loved to go to the library and borrow books, read for long hours in her room, and write poems as well as short stories. She was particularly good with computers at a young age. She designed our invitations for our anniversary celebration in February 1996. She enjoyed ballet dancing and celebrating her annual birthday party with family and friends.

In June 1996, Jo-An's progress at school came to a halt. During the spring of the school year, I met with Jo-An's teacher, who was at a loss to know how to get her focused again. She suggested a major task at school to encourage her involvement, so Jo-An's task was to ensure that everyone understood his or her part for a class play. Jo-An had informed me that she had misplaced the instructions. In April of 1996, I noticed the anxiety in her voice. I decided that we should call each student to explain his or her part. As we sat and called each student, I knew in my heart that Jo-An was experiencing something unusual. She was unable to finish her examinations by the end of the school year. Although she returned to school that September, it was obvious that by December, we were going to face the challenge of finding an alternative placement for her. Our journey with Jo-An was nonstop from that point on.

Our beautiful Jo-An needed a different type of care, care that was foreign to us. The lives of our entire family began to change. We did everything in our power to work at changing the situation, to make it right so we could be comfortable, but the situation never got better. In fact, it got worse. Tensions brewed in our home as the situation got worse, and I was pressed from every side to give up on Jo-An and to live my own life. But even in the midst of the pain, the stress, and the insecurity of life, God gave me strength for the journey ahead.

The months flew by, and my work was the only thing that kept me busy to pass the time and mask the pain. During my breaks, I was consumed with making appointments, talking to doctors, social workers, and school staff. I went home every day thinking and talking about the situations that confronted us. Jo-An was experiencing emotional upheaval. We did not have a clue how to help her. We relied on school personnel to guide us accordingly. This was new. Different. Scary.

20 Learning through Trials

Jo-An needed special care; we applied to a local hospital which had started an adolescent day program. We enrolled Jo-An in their day program from December 1996 to January 1997 before placing her in a special needs school in February of 1997. Carl and I alternated in getting her at the end of the day. Initially, all seemed to be going well. When she returned to the hospital between June and July 1997 for treatment, things had changed. We noticed our daughter was not speaking at all.

When Carl and I requested a team meeting, we found out that doctors had injected Jo-An, at age thirteen, with adult doses of Haldol medication, which we believe had debilitating effects on her brain, impairing her ability to communicate, write, or read. Our daughter looked weak, was not eating except when she was given tomato soup for dinner, and was not talking. We had meetings with the treatment team, who suggested that Jo-An be part of a study that the senior psychiatrist was conducting in Washington to find the drug that would benefit her. When we refused, the psychiatrist insisted on sending her to a state mental institution, telling us that she would never read or write, except color with crayons, at best. We wanted to take our daughter home by her birthday in September; when we realized that that was not going to happen, we secured a transfer to another hospital to obtain a second opinion.

The psychiatrist at the second hospital took her off her current medications to clean her system and to give her body time to adjust to new medications. However, after a month, he decided that Jo-An should be sent to a state mental institution and told us that if we did not comply with his recommendation, he would take us to court. He had given us information about a day treatment center, so on the eve of Jo-An's discharge, Carl and I urgently and quickly applied to this center, and Jo-An was accepted. The psychiatrist understood, I believe, our plight as parents, and decided not to take us to court.

In July 2000, when it seemed that our daughter's life was going downhill, I took a leave of absence from my new job after being there for four and a half years. My one-year leave turned into two and a half years. I was on a mission to help Jo-An, a mission that my family felt did not make practical sense. Our lives were in chaos. I felt alone. As my trials intensified, I had no other recourse but to pray, seek God's wisdom, wait on Him, and obey His voice. In August of 2000, I took our daughter off all the medications she was taking. The process was slow, and at times, I doubted whether I was doing the right thing, but as the months turned into years, Jo-An's health became stable. I replaced the medication with herbal therapy, which I had researched, and which included grape seed extract, flax seed, liquid B-complex vitamins, a liquid multivitamin, selenium, and ginkgo biloba. I mixed these into a smoothie with strawberries, seeds, walnuts, and lecithin. This she took daily. I made it a point to walk with Jo-An three times per week for fifteen minutes at a small park, which was not too busy and not too far from our home. It was not easy giving her walks. If I did not hold her hand and walk briskly, she would stop and pick up twigs and leaves, and our walking times would have been endless. I persevered.

Since my life was hectic, I woke up in the early morning hours and prayed to God in my home office. I cried, desperately asking God to heal our daughter, but nothing extraordinary resulted from my prayers. I was praying and crying out to God continuously. I was getting impatient with the situation before me and was wondering whether I would get any release. *Would I get help?* I was asking, "God, where are you in all of this?" I was in the greatest fire I had ever experienced, but I knew that God had promised to rescue me. I was asking, "How long, Lord? How long?"

We tried hospitalizations, a day treatment center, special schools, therapists, medication, but nothing worked. In August of 2000, on the advice of family and friends, I took Jo-An to a healing service at Worcester Centrum, where a leading evangelist was preaching. Jo-An got to the Centrum and sat quietly, but when she wanted to go to the restroom, I left my belongings with someone and proceeded to walk out of the aisle. In the space of one minute, Jo-An had disappeared, and I could not find her anywhere. I thought, *"What will Carl think of me if I return home without Jo-An?"*

I began to pray, "God, you are my present help in the time of trouble (Ps. 46:1). Lord, please show me where Jo-An is." I walked down the street, and there she was. I recognized her by the bright pink shirt she was wearing and by her tall, slender figure. I ran as fast as I could until I caught up with her. I held her hand, and, together, we walked back to the Centrum and onto the stage. Jo-An was not healed! I wanted to try everything, but I had taken a big step driving Jo-An to the Centrum and staying overnight in a hotel with her. I was desperate.

Notwithstanding, there continued to be challenging days ahead: getting Jo-An dressed in the mornings, getting her to the table on time for breakfast, preparing her lunch, and getting her to the waiting bus. Some days she boarded the bus; at other times, she did not. Every day was different. By the middle of March 2003, I had returned to work halftime and was getting full support from my husband, our two sons, and our older daughter. I was attending seminary classes twice per week at night, and although it was tiring to think of going to seminary classes after working for an entire day, once I got there, the atmosphere of prayer at the beginning of every class set the tone for the lively presentations and student interaction and support that I gladly received and welcomed. While I was enduring trials, God was doing a new thing by opening doors for me to attend seminary. I graduated in 2004.

As I reminisce, my greatest challenges were when I took Jo-An to her medical and dental appointments and had to wait in the waiting area. My worst nightmare was that she might get agitated, talk loudly, or throw a magazine on the floor, and then all eyes would be on us. Things have changed. Jo-An has come a long way. She can read and write. She attends a day-program where people are loving and happy. She has a personal dentist and feels loved every time she visits her. She behaves very well at the doctor's office. In fact, I rely on the community when I visit the hospital for her annual checkup. I recognize how much I can do by myself so Jo-An gets assistance from the MBTA ride so I do not have to park my car and experience difficulties. I also receive assistance from the medical team who helps her go to the bathroom. I also take Jo-An to the hospital cafeteria to get a bite following her appointment. Jo-An has continued to make slow and steady progress.

God had been continually at work in Jo-An's life, but we just could not see it. We wanted immediate results and could not fathom the depth of God's workmanship. We will never understand why Jo-An suffers with mental health issues or what God's will is for her life, but we know that God loves Jo-An, has created her in His own image and likeness, and has a perfect plan for her life as well as ours. God will unveil His plan for Jo-An when we wait patiently for it.

21 Example of God's Workmanship

Each of us can attest to God's workmanship in our lives. I have seen God work beautifully in our son Reese's life. I believe God has given him a gift of prophecy and I wait to see how that plays out in the future. He has also given him the gifts of love, patience, kindness, thoughtfulness, and compassion. It was God working through Reese to bring about these gifts. God can do the same for you.

Reese is friendly and kind to family and friends as well as to his customers at his barber salon as he listens to and gives advice regarding their life issues. At times, Reese will give free cuts to those who cannot afford to pay for them. He is always there when you need him and helps out in difficult situations. Sometimes, Carl and I may be having a challenging time with Jo-An and Reese visits us exactly when we need help. Reese is about family, making sure to take time to check in and see how his sister Jo-an, Carl, and I are doing, and when he visits us, he always gives Carl a haircut. From his youth, he had an ardent love for basketball and continues to play the game for strength training and to share and teach strategies of the game to others.

Reese has the favor of God. When he was four years old, he sat on my bed and listened as I read the Bible to him, and now, he is doing the same with his son. From time to time, we discuss the Bible and life issues, and he gives me a quotation from his library of quotations.

Recently, an organization with whom I am affiliated, honored me for Mother's Day. Reese took me to this event and brought me home. My son honored me that day and words cannot explain my gratitude to God. God is worthy to be praised and honored. We wait on God to do a work in us as well as in our children because we are His workmanship created in Christ Jesus for good works, which God prepared beforehand so that we would walk in them (Ephesians 2:10).

22 Standing on God's Promises

While my daughter's situation has not changed significantly, my journey with God has improved. My faith has increased, and I depend on Him for all things. Regardless of the outcomes, I wait on God for direction and hope, for in Him all things exist. He is the beginning and the ending, the author and finisher of my faith. Waiting on God allows me to witness God's mighty power, purpose, and plan for members of my family and for me. Oftentimes, we make decisions too quickly and miss out on what God is doing in that family member's life. God is almighty, He is powerful, and He can do all things and knows all things. He can change situations at the twinkle of an eye, and even if He does not, God knows best, and you and I must trust Him in all circumstances.

God is love and He showed his love to us when He sent his Son, Jesus Christ, to the world, to preach to the lost regarding the kingdom of God. Jesus shed his blood and rose the third day from the grave for our justification, for without the shedding of blood, no one can be justified in God's sight. When we confess and repent of our sins, ask God's forgiveness, and decide to accept Jesus as Lord and Savior of our lives, we receive the gift of salvation and eternal life. Now, God sees us as His sons and daughters, heirs, and joint heirs with Christ. God has forgiven us of our past, and even in the midst of turmoil, we can live a life of peace, joy, and hope, when we trust God and believe in Him.

While my life has been hectic dealing with my younger daughter, I continue to trust God and stand on His promises. I have not missed out on life as some people have thought, but, instead, I am happy, researching ways to help my daughter overcome her disability, happy that I have returned to my writing and my YouTube channel activities. I give my God thanks in all circumstances for this is His will concerning me. God is not finished with me yet; I am thankful for the life He has given me and will continue to work in His kingdom, bringing the lost to a saving knowledge of Christ.

Surrendering All To Christ

In June 2002, I was at Yarmouth on my yearly retreat to rest and reassess my life. I checked into a hotel at 3 p.m. that afternoon, rested a bit, and had dinner about 7 p.m. The fish dinner was not that great. I have had better. The restaurant was a bit noisy and crowded too. Not having my car limited me to nearby restaurants; however, I enjoyed walking and viewing scenic Cape Cod. I bought juice and a piece of fruit for my evening snack and proceeded to my hotel room. That night, I began reviewing my journals from 1983 onward.

I perused my journals quickly. The first portion of my journals revealed that I was frustrated at times, wanting my freedom and complete control of my life, and when I did not get what I wanted, it seemed that I resorted to being rebellious toward God, my Father, despite all that He continued to do for me. I was praying for God to give me things and change my circumstances but never asking God for His will to be done. I was angry and frustrated, blaming my husband when problems arose instead of praying to God about the situation and leaving it in His hands. I devoted many years to inner struggles rather than focusing on God's purpose for my life.

I continued to peruse these pages the next morning on a lawn chair at the makeshift beach at the rear of the hotel. I could see the bay ahead. The skies were blue, the air fresh, and the sun shining. *"Surely this is the way to enjoy life, even temporarily,"* I thought.

The Holy Spirit revealed to me who I was. I recognized my sins of disobedience, pride, control, rebellion, unforgiveness, insecurity, fear, and procrastination, asked God's forgiveness, and promised to utterly depend on Him. I confirmed God's love for me, noting that He wanted the best for me, His best. I asked God to guide and direct me and to provide me with what I needed rather than what I wanted. I asked that my life be lived for His glory only. At that retreat, the Lord was instructing me to surrender all to Him.

24 Depending Totally on God

Since 1990, I had been telling God all my problems, angered at how long I had to wait on Him, angry at the situation I was in, doing everything but realizing that it was time to wait. It was time to change my ways.

In the spring of 1999, I enrolled at a local seminary taking my first class in Church Management. Carl supported me in that effort, caring for Jo-An while I attended classes. The class taught me all aspects of church management, from organizing Bible studies to writing church newsletters. I was always interested in writing when I was a teenager, so the idea of creating a newsletter was fascinating to me. God was giving me the signal to move without doubt. I proceeded to produce my first issue, which was published in the fall of 1999.

In the summer of 1999, during my personal retreat on the Cape, I was praying for family needs. Two months later, in November of 1999, Jo-An was being transferred to another hospital, so I was experiencing more trials. During this period, I listened to the voice of God and constantly and consistently recorded in my journals a Scripture verse that came to mind at that moment concerning the issue for which I was praying. God repeatedly showed me that He was my Shepherd (Psalm 23), that He would deliver me from my fears (Ps.34:4), and that His word would not go void (Is.55:11). I could count on God to come through for me when no one else would. God knew the inside scoop of my life, the difficulties I was encountering. I was trapped in my own prison of hopelessness, praying, and waiting for the Master to open the prison gate.

My life continued to move in a downhill and, sometimes, in an uphill spiral. Some days seemed to pass me by without my completing a task. I prayed but did not always get a chance to read my Bible. I was forever cleaning and cooking. It seemed that I was in a constant battle for survival, but God was with me. One day in November, I poured my heart out to God. I cried, because I knew He had kept me from the pangs of death in years past by healing my illnesses and that He had promised to do it again.

In the midst of my hardship, caring for Jo-An, and having the load of running the house, I was excited about classes, the people with whom I was meeting, and the research papers that I was writing. I was stretched to the maximum with seminary studies. By December 4, 2001, I wanted to give up, but God answered my prayer.

I wrote these words in my journal:

> God continued to move me to the next level and gave me strength to persevere through the storms. I thanked God for allowing me to have a husband who is a great provider and who supported me as I moved forward. I continued to depend on God for my every need, reminding Him of His promises to heal our daughter Jo-An. In December 2001, I was ready to consecrate my life to God. I asked Him to change me and use me. I admitted I was willing to please Him for the rest of my life. I was willing to receive His courage and strength, and to give love to His people. I asked God to take away my weaknesses and allow His grace to be sufficient for me. I realized that I was privileged to receive the seconds, minutes, hours, days, weeks, months, and years that God had given me and that I was not thanking Him enough for what He had done and continued to do for me. I was complaining. I refused to wait. I wanted answers quickly. But who am I? I am a child of God. God is God, and He will always be in control.

Yes, God was in charge of my life and was leading me, although I could not see it physically. He continued to bring Scriptures to my heart after my daily prayers. By the middle of December 2001, I noted good things happening in my household. Jo-An cried out one day and said, "Lord, have mercy." My job had approved another year of family medical leave for me. I had experienced God's love in the midst of the battle that was raging in my life. I really believed that things did not happen by chance and that Jo-An's situation had taught me to look at life differently.

I was returning from doing some errands on Thursday, September 9, 2004, when my life changed for the worse. I was happy that I had purchased cable and Internet services. I was reviewing the cable on the outside of the house. As I left the car, the car began to roll down the driveway toward another car which was parked across the street. I tried to stop it and landed on my face, damaging my knees. The car hit one parked car, and, luckily, no one was hurt. Two people drove by slowly as they saw what was happening, got out of their cars, and went to get me some help. With blood gushing from my knees and in excruciating pain, I stood up, relieved that my face was not torn, walked inside, and changed my clothes. Within five minutes, the police had come to my assistance, had taken a report, and had called an ambulance to take me to a nearby hospital.

The night seemed long as I went through various tests to check for broken bones and fractures. Next came the cleaning and stitching of the deeper wounds. Ouch! That was painful! It hurt badly, even when I was given pain relievers. I was allergic to morphine and vomited excessively. Monique was there at my side and stayed with me until I was ready to go home. Carl stayed at home with Jo-An.

Monique came by that Friday and the week following to help get Jo-An on the bus. She brought me food that Saturday afternoon. Carl was also helpful in the mornings before he left for work. In the days and weeks following, I suffered with pain: it was painful getting off my bed, walking downstairs, going outside, and standing at the bottom of the driveway to get Jo-An off the bus in the afternoons. I felt lonely lying on the bed from day to day, having to help myself and Jo-An, who relied on me totally. It was difficult!

As I later reviewed the events of that week, I began to thank God for His mighty hands upon my life. I thanked Him for His greatness, His loving kindness, and His mercy toward me. His hands of mercy had pulled me up from the ground and allowed me to walk into our home to change my clothes. God had sent strangers to assist in getting an ambulance to take me to the hospital. He had sent doctors and nurses to help me throughout the night. I was thankful to God for my husband Carl and for our daughter Monique. God had sent the Holy Spirit to comfort me through the pain and the difficult nights that I experienced. The Lord had used this time to give me a chance to rest, pray, and seek Him.

God showed me how much He loved me and how He had forgiven me of all my sins. He assured me that He was in the business of restoring His servants to wholeness, and that He is a God of second chances.

25 Growing in Faith

If anyone had asked me twelve or more years ago what I would have done about my situation, it would definitely not be the same answer that I would give today. My situation has changed a little, but the major changes have come from within my heart. God continues to work in me. Years ago, I was not dependent on God and was operating on my own strength. That brought on tiredness, doubts, and fears. When I turned to trusting God about Jo-An, and took little steps getting help with her care, God gave me the strength to take bigger ones. Also, when I viewed Jo-An's situation differently, as a gift and not as a burden, things took a different turn. Granted, each day was different. Some days I would talk about my troubles; other days I would not. However, I began to yield to God's plans and wishes to love and help Jo-An because she was one of His chosen daughters. Every day I wake up—I thank God for giving me life. God has sent some help my way, but the bulk of the responsibility still rests on Carl and me as parents.

In the meantime, I am concentrating on knowing my purpose and helping others. I understand now, that over the past years, God was guiding, upholding, and giving me strength through His Word, which was all on which I could depend. No one understood my pain, my suffering, or my frustration. God did. He was molding and shaping me into the person He wanted me to be—loving, kind, faithful, and compassionate to others. He was establishing me, building my character, giving me wisdom and patience, healing my fears and my brokenness, bringing me closer to Him, and showing me that my focus was to be on Him, not on my problems.

Most of all, He wanted me to live a life of faith and trust in Him. I am growing in faith because God is in control of my life, helping me every step of the way. He has taught me through trials and waits to see if I will pass every test, so I can be elevated to the next level. Because of this, I refuse to bathe myself in self-defeat or self-pity. I have decided to take this faith-walk regardless of my circumstances; this faith-walk is based on a relationship between God and me. I have purposed to take God at His word and invest my time living a life of faith and resting in God's everlasting arms.

26 Celebrating My Life and Thanking God for It

As a family, we had cookouts to celebrate Memorial Day as well as christenings, birthdays, and graduations. We also had retirement parties, weddings, and our wedding anniversary at other venues, but none of our previous celebrations left an impression on our minds like the celebration of my life and my birthday, which took place on November 16, 2024.

Preparation for the celebration of my life event was extremely important and at first appeared stressful, for I was looking at the entire picture and felt that I could not put this together. I booked a party planner who ended up being expensive and wanted to work on the event program immediately, making me feel rushed and uncomfortable. My daughter Monique used Canva.com and created a beautiful program for me. I worked on the centerpieces myself, buying silk flowers from an online store, purchasing vases from an art store, and ordering the rocks for the vases from Amazon. After cutting the stems to fit the vases, Monique assembled the flowers in each vase.

Later, I secured the cake from a bakery near our home, ordered inflated balloons, and had both the balloons and the cake delivered to the venue in Quincy, MA. The DJ we previously hired changed his payment amount at the last minute, so I secured another DJ who was far easier to work with and had a great selection of music.

We also received a call from the photographer, who canceled his engagement. That same week, I got a call from my niece who I paid to set up a photo booth so everyone could have fun taking pictures of themselves and/or their families. God was orchestrating this party as everything was falling into place and everyone had a part to play.

Our guests were mainly family members and a few friends. Family members included our adult children, our six grandchildren, my three sisters, my brother, a cousin, a host of nieces and nephews, their spouses and their children, Carl's brother, his two nephews, a spouse, and two nieces who flew in from Georgia, Michigan, Pennsylvania, and New Jersey to be a part of this celebration. Carl's family members as well as mine were happy to come together for this time of celebration and reunion, having experienced the deaths of several family members during the past three years. They also knew of our struggles with Jo-An and were glad to see her.

Jo-An, her personal care attendant who was dressed beautifully, Carl, and I attended the event together. It was comforting having someone help Jo-An so we could relax. The attendant was excellent; she came on time to the house to dress Jo-An bringing her additional makeup, a black purse, and a headband. Jo-An looked beautiful in her blue flowered dress that fitted her exactly right over her knees and the blue head band was just the right color. Carl wore a light grey, well-fitted suit with a black tie. I wore a dress that I bought two years ago and never wore from monies that our daughter Monique had given me for Christmas. It was a navy blue laced dress, with lots of sparkles fitting just over my knees. I wore matching earrings. I also wore a beautiful matching necklace and bracelet that my son Reese had given me as gifts.

The mood of the event was celebration and joy. Everyone was happy to see each other. Everyone was smiling, laughing, singing, eating, speaking to each other, hugging each other, dancing, or taking photos. The food was exceptional: fish, chicken, rice, vegetables, and a salad. Our daughter Monique prepared a movie showing pictures of me at different stages of my life to the amazement of the audience. My son Tony did a great job as MC for a short period of time, while my daughter Monique took over for the rest of the night, putting order to the event and organizing additional speakers who gave tributes during dessert. DJ Kriss' music added to the mood and joy of the event. He played the gospel tunes of my choice as well as his own music.

The program began with Pastor Maxie of New Beginning Church of God, who described me as a woman of God and spoke to my children regarding who I am and then gave a moving prayer. I was thrilled to hear from my husband, who spoke about me as a religious person, and our adult children, who spoke from their hearts about how I was an encouraging mother. My grandson Reesey said kind words about me as well. I was next in line to give a thank you message to the audience.

What I conveyed in my message was the greatness of God and how He has impacted my life. I thanked God for giving me life, for carrying me through life, for His healing power, for giving me strength in times of weakness, for loving and forgiving me through all my failures. I thanked God for giving me a second chance, for establishing me, and giving me the faith to stand strong and the hope to believe in Him for all things that relate to life and godliness.

I thanked God for my husband, who has remained loving, patient, supportive in both joyful and challenging times. I thanked God for my amazing children: for Monique for her love, kindness, and generosity over the years. She has stood by my side in joyful and challenging times and has supported me in all aspects of my ministry. I thanked God for Jo-An, who allowed me to understand God's workmanship in me. I thanked God for Reese, who loves and adores family and is always there in times of need. I thanked God for Tony, our older son, for his love, kindness, and willingness to help in times of need. I thanked God for my daughter-in-law for her love and compassion for family and her support during my ministry and my son-in-law for his love and kindness stepping in when Carl and I were ill, giving us advice and preparing food for us. Lastly, I thanked God for my six grandchildren and the immense joy that they have brought me.

I continued by thanking God for extended family members and friends who supported Carl and me on our journey. I reminded family and friends of the times we went from house to house praying for each other and the times they gathered at our home for cookouts, christenings, birthdays, graduations, and at other venues for weddings and other events. I reminisced of the times when I sat at their tables eating delicious meals and discussing life, the times that we gathered for tea or for banquets. I was grateful to many of them who supported me in my personal life and ministry, standing with me in prayer and in support groups, attending or hosting my conferences, and allowing me to preach, conduct workshops, and women's retreats. I explained that those opportunities that I received when I was a member of a church, impacted my life profoundly and were instrumental in shaping my life to do God's will and to show others how great God is and how much He loves us all. I encouraged the attendees and you, my readers, to press on as I have, with resounding faith that never fails, regardless of the challenges you face. Remember, God knows all about you and loves you. He has a plan for your life and will guide you through it as He has guided me.

The night was moving fast. Our personal care attendant had done an excellent job so far, making sure Jo-An took photos with cousins at the photo booth and that Jo-An did not make noise at the table. After dinner, it was time to consider calling an Uber to pick up our daughter Jo-An and her personal care attendant to take them home.

During dessert, Monique began organizing family members and friends who wanted to pay tributes. My friend joked about the times we had living together with other women at a residence and whenever she looked in the lobby, Carl was always there. My friend who we regard as family and my friend who I met at the residence, also remarked on the times we had together. My brother remembered times at our parents' home in Trinidad when I prepared turkey and other foods on special occasions, and how I have not changed, and have always brought family together. My youngest sister explained how she would entrust me with personal information, and I would never share it. Two of my nieces and my cousin explained how they felt comfortable speaking with me about any issue. Carl's older niece explained that when she was a little girl, Carl would take her to my mother's home and she would sit in the living room and listen to conversations. She explained that Carl and I were inseparable: "When you saw Carl, you saw Joan." We heard from Carl's other family members, his niece, who sang an inspirational song to me and his nephew, who was very encouraging.

Pastor Maxie's wife shared that she was especially grateful for the prayers I prayed for her children and that she believed God brought us together as friends. I truly believe that as well because Pastor Maxie and his wife hosted our first Christian Resource Network Conference in 2002, and we developed a meaningful friendship, supporting each other through prayer.

After leaving the party with a large bouquet of flowers that I received from my brother, his wife, and daughter, and lugging all of that into the car, Carl and I went to the supermarket and bought flour to make homemade bread for our family and Carl's for the next day, as we had invited them over to spend the day with us. We had a wonderful time discussing different issues and bonding together.

I will never forget how happy I was at that party, but I pray that you and I will always be happy because of the goodness of God. I pray that God will continue to bless you and help you when you go through a difficult time. I pray that God will break every stronghold that is preventing you from moving forward.

I thank the following people: my husband, Carl, for his financial support, Monique for dedicating her time and resources to preparing the slide-show and serving as MC, our sons, Tony, and Reese, in their roles as MC, my grandson, Reesey, who danced with me, as well as family and friends who gave speeches, captured moments through photos and videos and blessed me with thoughtful gifts. I will always be grateful for the love and support they have shown me.

I pray in the name of Jesus, that God will set you free in every area of your life so you can walk boldly in your purpose. May His goodness and mercy follow you always.

Legacy & Reflections

Table of Contents for Legacy and Reflections

Introduction

As this book ends, I want to leave you with something more that extends beyond my personal journey. This section, *Legacy and Reflections,* is a space for wisdom, encouragement, and faith to live on. It is a collection of memories, heartfelt letters, cherished scriptures, and meaningful quotes that I hope will inspire you in your own walk-through life.

Within these pages, you will find personal reflections on faith, perseverance, and gratitude—lessons that have shaped my journey and may offer guidance for yours. You will read about treasured family moments that remind us of the beauty of love and resilience. Through letters to my children, grandchildren, caregivers, and those facing challenges, I share words of hope and encouragement meant to uplift future generations. The selected Bible verses serve as reminders of God's unwavering presence, while the quotations offer wisdom drawn from scripture and personal experience.

My hope is that this section not only adds depth to the book but also provides you with inspiration to reflect on your own legacy—what you will leave behind for those who come after you. May these words bring comfort, encouragement, and a renewed sense of faith as you continue your journey.

Why I Wrote this Book

Courtesy: Andrew Heel • Unsplash

I wrote this book to give you hope as you go through your struggles. My journey as a wife and mother has been difficult at times, but I am happy to say that with the help of God, I was able to make it successfully because of the commitment I made to my family and to God. Journaling helped me during my journey; it allowed me to understand how I felt during difficult times and how I could change my feelings, depend on God more, and know God's purpose for my life.

Everyone has a purpose and sometimes we go through struggles to reach our purpose. We must pray and believe God for the utmost. In doing so, our situation changes for the better. God loves us, his children, and promises never to leave or forsake us, but to give us the strength as we go through struggles, and to supply our needs according to His riches in glory by Christ Jesus.

Lessons on Faith and Perseverance

Courtesy: Peter Vanosdall • Unsplash

Through the many challenges that I have experienced, I learned to embrace faith. I learned that when you apply faith, God uses your faith to give you more opportunities because you have shown bravery in your circumstances so God can move you to the next level. When you pray and communicate with God, he hears and answers your cries, he delivers you from your perils and plants your feet on solid ground. This is in keeping with the statement: Ask and you shall receive, knock, and the door shall be opened unto you.

The Power of Gratitude and Grace

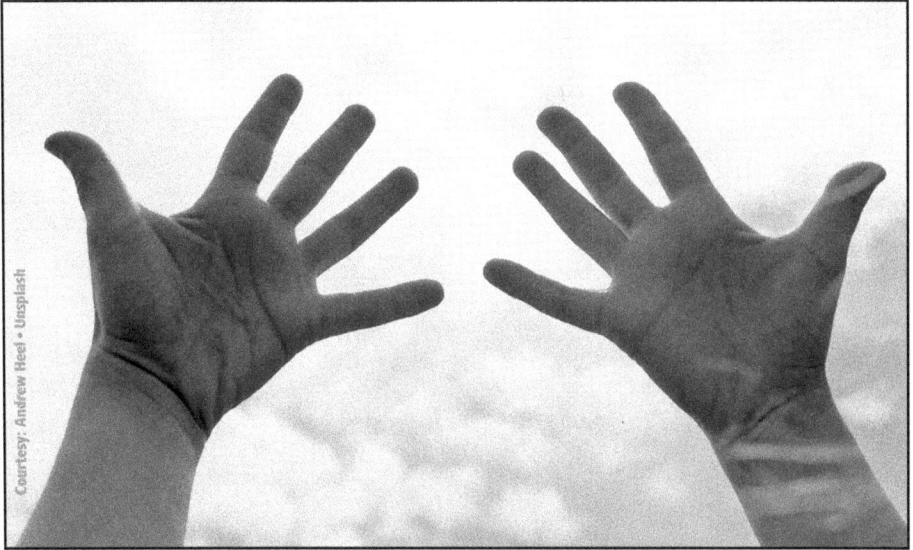

Courtesy: Andrew Heel • Unsplash

I learned from my journey that it is by grace that you and I have been saved. It was not based on our works; but on the sacrifice that Jesus Christ made by dying on the cross for our sins. Because of the power of Grace, God shows his love, kindness, and faithfulness to you and to me. I have accepted Christ to be my Lord and Savior, renounced and asked God for forgiveness for all of my sins. Now, I have a relationship with Jesus Christ, my Lord, and my Savior, and have the assurance of salvation and the gift of eternal life.

Waiting on God's Timing

During my life's journey, I have learned to trust God's timing. We must remember that we are God's children, and He is our Father and He knows what is best for us. When we are going through storms in our lives, God is testing and proving us to see if we could pass the test. God knows when to remove the test or when to move us to the next level. He is the author and finisher of our faith, the beginning and ending, and knows what is best for us.

Closing Reflection

Courtesy: José M. Reyes • Unsplash

This book is more than my story—it is a testimony of faith, perseverance, and God's unwavering grace. My hope is that as you read these pages, you will be reminded that no matter what trials you face, you are never alone. May my journey inspire you to hold on to faith, embrace, hope, and walk confidently in your purpose.

A Vacation to Remember

Courtesy: David Clode • Unsplash

I remember the green car we had; we called it the "Green Machine." It broke down every time my husband Carl took us somewhere. We were thinking about going to Portland Maine to board the Scotia Prince one day in 1986. Were we out of our minds? What if the car broke down with all of us in it? How would we get around? We knew no one in Maine. However, God was with us, and we were on time to board the boat with our vehicle. When we got to Nova Scotia, our daughter needed to go to the bathroom, we knocked on the door of a stranger and she opened the door for us. Our children loved the vacation, they swam in the pond nearby, walked, rode their bicycles, and we had a wonderful vacation—one we would always remember.

The Day that Changed Everything

Courtesy: Igor Oliyarnik • Unsplash

The day that changed everything was when Carl and I got married. Later, we had children and we celebrated our wedding anniversary, our children's birthday parties, and graduations. We had many cookouts and celebrations which continued for many years—and now, our children celebrate our grandchildren's birthdays, and we are getting ready to celebrate our grandson's graduation.

Letter to My Children

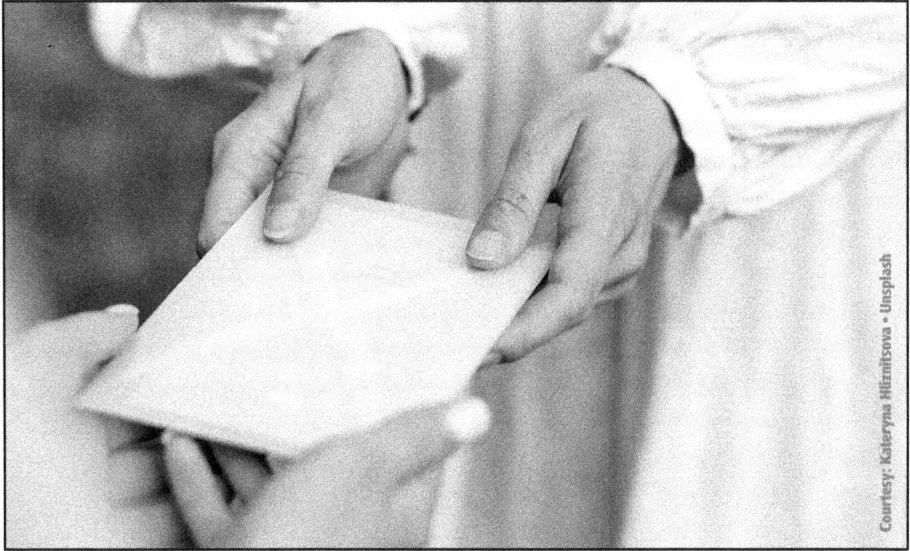

Courtesy: Kateryna Hliznitsova • Unsplash

L ife is a journey of faith, perseverance, and grace. As you go through challenges, remember that God is always with you. There will be moments of doubt, but never forget that you were created with a purpose. Be transformed by the renewing of your mind so you will be able to evaluate and approve what God's will is for your life. Love one another the same way God loves you; never feel you are better than someone else. Live in peace with everyone and pray to God consistently for guidance, healing, restoration, and answers to your life's problems.

This book is a keepsake that I hope will remind you of the strength that runs through our family. No matter what you face, hold on to faith, and trust that God's timing is always perfect.

With love and blessings, Mom...

Letter to My Dear Grandchildren

Courtesy: Shiv Singh • Unsplash

As you grow and walk through life's challenges, I want you to remember this: God loves you; you are fearfully and wonderfully made, and God has a plan for you—and his plan is for your good so you can choose to be your best because God expects that of you. Know that God is always with you wherever you go, and you can pray to him when you need guidance. Be humble, loving, and be kind to others. I have walked through trials, but I depend on God's promises to carry me through. You too, will find strength in His grace.

With love and blessings, Grandma...

A Letter of Encouragement To those Who Struggle

Courtesy: Asfand Yar • Unsplash

I do not know what you are struggling with, but I want you to know that God loves you and has a plan and purpose for your life. His plan is to prosper you and not to harm you, but to give you hope and a future. Activate your faith in God when you are struggling; replace fear with faith which will help you to achieve the plans God has for you, for God has not given you a spirit of fear but of power, and of love, and a sound mind.

God wants you to be strong, courageous, and not to be fearful and dismayed, for He will be with you wherever you go. Never give up; press on to the high calling of God in Christ Jesus until you attain your goals.

To Fellow Caregivers

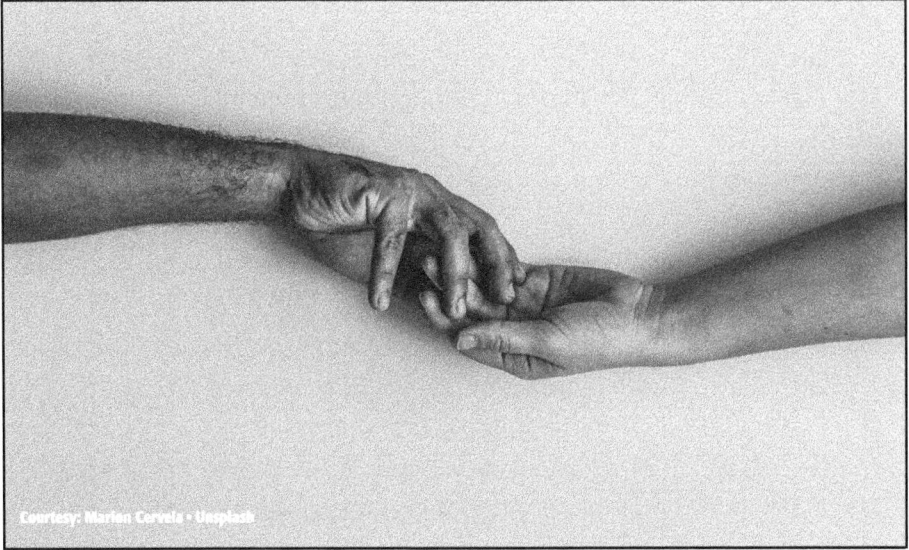

Courtesy: Marion Cervela • Unsplash

To all my fellow caregivers who struggle daily, I understand how you feel, but most of all, God does, and He gives you the strength to go through every difficulty that life poses. Trust God when you are experiencing difficulties and remember not to become weary in doing good, for at the proper time you will reap a harvest if you do not give up.

Words of Wisdom for The Next Generation

Courtesy: Martin Olsson • Unsplash

I know it is difficult for you to look ahead and realize the importance of having a relationship with God because you feel you cannot detach yourselves from the ways of the world, but I want to leave you with words of wisdom.

God loves you at your worst moment. When you are going through difficulties, God never forsakes you. He is with you at all times and in all situations. Trust God, and regardless of your age, join forces with God and live a life of faith, grounded in the knowledge of God. It was by mere love that God sacrificed his Son on the cross for you. Accept Jesus Christ as Lord and Savior, confess and ask forgiveness for your sin, and you will receive salvation and eternal life.

Finding Strength in Difficult Times

Courtesy: Cristian Lozan • Unsplash

1 **Isaiah 41:10**—Fear not, for I am with you; be not dismayed, for I am your God; I will strengthen you, I will help you, I will uphold you with my righteous right hand.

2 **Philippians 4:13**—I can do all things through Christ who strengthens me.

3 **2 Corinthians 12:9–10**—But he said to me, 'My grace is sufficient for you, for my power is made perfect in weakness.'

4 **Psalm 46:1**—God is our refuge and strength, a very present help in trouble.

5 **Deuteronomy 31:6**—Be strong and courageous. Do not fear or be in dread of them, for it is the Lord your God who goes with you. He will not leave you or forsake you.

6 **Psalm 34:17–18**—The righteous cry out, and the Lord hears them; he delivers them from all their troubles. The Lord is close to the brokenhearted and saves those who are crushed in spirit.

7 **Joshua 1:9**—Have I not commanded you? Be strong and courageous. Do not be frightened, and do not be dismayed, for the Lord your God is with you wherever you go.

8 **Exodus 15:2**—The Lord is my strength and my song, and he has become my salvation; this is my God, and I will praise him, my father's God, and I will exalt him.

9 **Psalm 55:22**—Cast your burden on the Lord, and he will sustain you; he will never permit the righteous to be moved.

10 **Isaiah 40:29–31**—He gives power to the faint, and to him who has no might he increases strength. Even youths shall faint and be weary, and young men shall fall exhausted; but they who wait for the Lord shall renew their strength; they shall mount up with wings like eagles; they shall run and not be weary; they shall walk and not faint.

God's Grace in Every Season

1 Lamentations 3:22–23—The steadfast love of the Lord never ceases; his mercies never come to an end; they are new every morning; great is your faithfulness.

2 2 Corinthians 9:8—And God is able to make all grace abound to you, so that having all sufficiency in all things at all times, you may abound in every good work.

3 Ephesians 2:8–9—For by grace you have been saved through faith, and this is not your own doing; it is the gift of God, not a result of works, so that no one may boast.

4 Titus 2:11–12—For the grace of God has appeared, bringing salvation for all people, training us to renounce ungodliness and worldly passions, and to live self-controlled, upright, and godly lives in the present age.

5 Romans 5:1–2—Therefore, since we have been justified by faith, we have peace with God through our Lord Jesus Christ. Through him we have also obtained access by faith into this grace in which we stand, and we rejoice in hope of the glory of God.

6 **Acts 20:32**—Now I commit you to God and to the word of his grace, which can build you up and give you an inheritance among all those who are sanctified.

7 **Hebrews 4:16**—Let us then approach God's throne of grace with confidence, so that we may receive mercy and find grace to help us in our time of need.

8 **James 4:6**—But he gives more grace. Therefore, it says, "God opposes the proud but gives grace to the humble."

9 **John 3:16**—For God so loved the world, that he gave his only Son, that whoever believes in him should not perish but have eternal life.

10 **1 Peter 4:10**—Each of you should use whatever gift you have received to serve others, managing it wisely, as a good steward of God's grace in its various forms.

Standing on His Promises

Courtesy: Alfonso Betancourt • Unsplash

1 **Proverbs 3:5–6**—Trust in the Lord with all your heart, and do not lean on your own understanding. In all your ways acknowledge him, and he will make straight your paths.

2 **Numbers 23:19**—God is not a man, that he should lie, or a son of man, that he should change his mind. Has he said, and will he not do it? Or has he spoken, and will he not fulfill it?

3 **2 Peter 1:3-4**—His divine power has granted to us all things that pertain to life and godliness, through the knowledge of him who called us to his own glory and excellence, by which he has granted to us his precious and very great promises.

4 **Jeremiah 29:11**—For I know the plans I have for you, declares the Lord, plans for welfare and not for evil, to give you a future and a hope.

5 **Hebrews 10:23**—Let us hold fast the confession of our hope without wavering, for he who promised is faithful.

6 **2 Chronicles 20:15**—Do not be afraid or discouraged because of this vast army. For the battle is not yours, but God's.

7 **Psalm 138:3**—On the day I called, you answered me; my strength of soul you increased.

8 **Nehemiah 8:10**—Do not grieve, for the joy of the Lord is your strength.

9 **Romans 8:28**—And we know that in all things God works for the good of those who love him, who have been called according to his purpose.

10 **1 Peter 5:10**   And after you have suffered a little while, the God of all grace, who has called you to his eternal glory in Christ, will himself restore, confirm, strengthen, and establish you.

Meaningful Verses

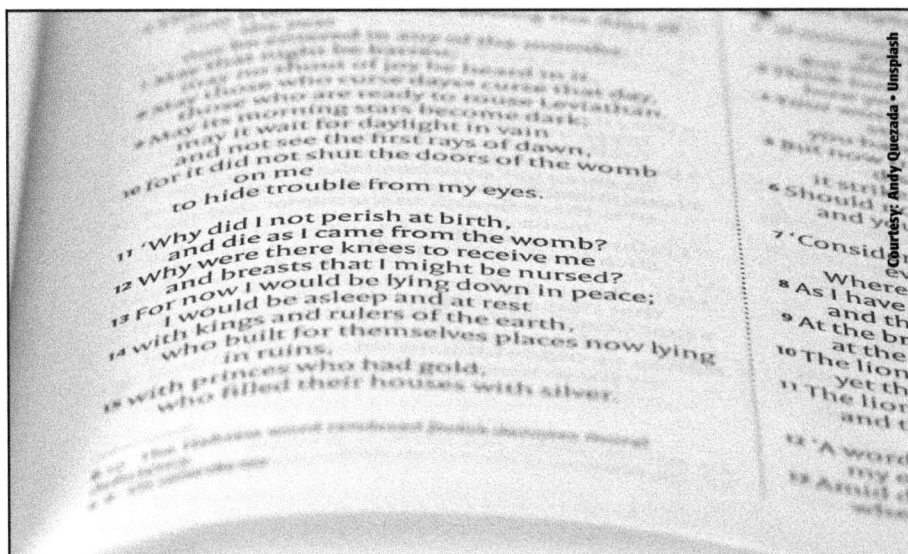

Courtesy: Andy Quezada • Unsplash

- But the plans of the Lord stand firm forever, the purposes of his heart through all generations. —**Psalm 33:11**

- You may not know what tomorrow holds, but you can trust the One who holds tomorrow.

- Your trials are not the end of your story—they are the beginning of your testimony.

- A life rooted in faith will always bear fruit in due season.

- the Lord is my light and my salvation; whom shall I fear? The Lord is the stronghold of my life; of whom shall I be afraid? —**Psalm 27:1**

Scripture-Based Quotes

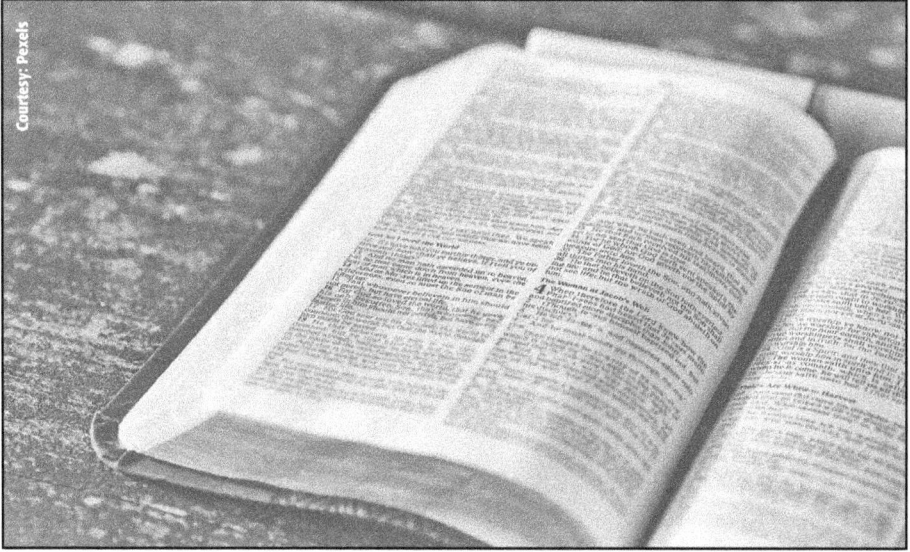

Courtesy: Pexels

- The Lord is my strength and my shield; my heart trusts in Him, and He helps me. —**Psalm 28:7**

- God is within her, she will not fall; God will help her at break of day. —**Psalm 46:5**

- When you go through deep waters, I will be with you. —**Isaiah 43:2**

- For the Spirit God gave us does not make us timid, but gives us power, love, and self-discipline. —**2 Timothy 1:7**

- And so we know and rely on the love God has for us. God is love. Whoever lives in love lives in God, and God in them. —**I John 4:16**

Personal Wisdom and Encouragement

- No matter how hard the journey is, always keep your faith. It will lead you where you need to go.

- Your past does not define you; God's grace does.

- Walk in faith, not fear. The road ahead may be unknown, but God has already gone before you.

- Even in the storm, God is working. Trust His timing.

- Be a light wherever you go. The kindness you show today may change someone's tomorrow.

- You are never alone. God's hand is always guiding you.

- The love you give will outlive you—leave a legacy of faith, kindness, and courage.

- Success is not measured by wealth but by the lives you touch.

- Hold on to hope; it is the anchor of your soul.

- Never fear, but know that God has given you power, love, and a sound mind.

- Always remember you can do all things in Christ who gives you strength.

- Aim to become a better person in your life, be humble and kind to others.

- All life-Issues can be solved; it depends on how you go about solving them.

- Know that all things are possible with God; never underestimate yourself and your capabilities.

- Be patient with your children and have faith that God will change them one day.

- Pray without ceasing and God will help you as you solve your problems.

- God does not judge you based on what you have done or if you have failed; God loves You even when you are at your worst moment.

- Thank God for life, zeal, for plenty, for little; thank Him in every situation for this is His will concerning you.

Stay Connected with Joan M. Blake

Thank you for reading

Standing on His Promises—Then and Now.

To continue your journey of faith and healing:

- Visit **www.joanmblake.com** for blogs, upcoming events, and additional resources.

- Subscribe to **www.YouTube.com/@joanMBlak**e for weekly videos and teachings.

- Subscribe to **YouTube, Apple, Spotify,** and other platforms for the *Insights on Healing Podcast.*

Join our community and stay inspired!

www.ingramcontent.com/pod-product-compliance
Lightning Source LLC
Chambersburg PA
CBHW040803150426
42811CB00082B/2380/J